No. 25538/G.S.M.T.2 (P).

MGS-A 250 (N).
60,000

Motto

Whenever we speak and think of the great captains, and set up our military altars to Hannibal and Napoleon and Marlborough and such-like, let us add one more altar, "To the Unknown Leader", that is, to the good company, platoon, or section leader who carries forward his men or holds his post....

It is these who in the end do most to win wars.

Lord Wavell

The Naval & Military Press Ltd

Published by

The Naval & Military Press Ltd

Unit 5 Riverside, Brambleside
Bellbrook Industrial Estate
Uckfield, East Sussex
TN22 1QQ England

Tel: +44 (0)1825 749494

www.naval-military-press.com
www.nmarchive.com

Contents

Part One: Operational Notes

Special Features.

Part Two: Useful Things to Know.

Part Three: Jungle Lanes

Appendix

No. 25   JULY 1944

PART ONE

OPERATIONAL NOTES

1. ATTACK BY INFILTRATION

1. Operations in ASSAM and the ARAKAN have demonstrated that the formal frontal infantry attack supported by a barrage and made against organized Japanese positions is rarely effective and often costly.

2. The reasons for this are :

(a) The artillery fire can seldom be sufficiently heavy to destroy. At the best, therefore, it can only achieve neutralization.

(b) The value of support by neutralization is dependent on the ability of the infantry to enter the position before the effect of neutralization wears off. This is a matter of careful timing. Accurate timing is almost impossible owing to :

(i) The difficulty of assessing accurately speed of the movement on steep gradients and through thick jungle.

(ii) Restricted visibility, which makes artillery control by observation unreliable.

(c) The loss of surprise by reason of preliminary bombardment and attack from the expected direction.

3. Whilst superiority of fire and numbers are important assets in jungle fighting, it is infiltration and encirclement by skilful infantry led by good junior leaders, which will pay the highest dividends.

4. Without good patrolling, infiltration is impossible. It is patrols who provide the information on which infiltration is planned and develops.

Recce patrols should be small—NOT more than 2 or 3 men under an officer or NCO. If they are to operate at such a distance from our own positions that an advanced base is necessary from which they can go forward to get the information required, then a sub-unit of anything from a platoon to a company may be necessary to form this patrolling base.

Fighting patrols should normally be NOT less than a platoon and may be up to one company. Their main tasks are to " see off " enemy patrols, to lay ambushes based on information brought in by recce patrols, and to exploit forward to seize important tactical features on the next "bound" of our advance.

5. It is a mistake however to consider that infiltration tactics can only be employed by small forces or in close country. The Japanese and General Wingate have provided examples of the infiltration of large forces in jungle, and the following two examples from actions of the 4th Indian Division in North Africa admirably exemplify the technique of infiltration tactics in open country.

In February 1942, a Brigade of the 4th Indian Division was told to send a party out to pass through the German army and to destroy enemy aircraft on the Martuba airfield, 50 miles away. 2/5 Mahrattas sent an officer with 8 men of their long range platoon, with a couple of Indian sappers, in two trucks to do the job. This party slipped through the Germans at night, and with their trucks camouflaged in a wadi, lay up for two nights and days in the middle of the hostile army, reconnoitring the airfield. On the third night they passed on foot through the airfield defences and while the infantry blew up the aircraft the sappers destroyed the bomb dump. They then drove back through the German armoured divisions. An infantry patrol on an infantry job.

At Wadi Akarit in early April, 1943, it seemed impossible to get into the precipitous Zouai Hills held by the enemy. Perhaps the Germans thought so too. But a patrol of the 2nd Gurkhas worked into the position and found a gap in the enemy defences and a way up the precipice that led into the heart of the position, and so to the tops of the dominating hills. On a dark night the battalion quietly slipped through this gap company by company, the platoons working outwards to right and left inside the position. By 0200 hrs. they had reached the dominating hills and were killing everything they could find. The Sussex passed through the gaps the Gurkhas had made and worked out still wider to the North, and with a series of rapid assaults, seized the vital heights to protect the flank of the Northumbrian Division. 16th Punjab Regiment did the same to the South, and by dawn the 7th Indian Brigade had " opened up " the position to over 2,000 yards in depth. Then 5th Indian Brigade, infiltrating boldly through, rapidly secured the whole position. The armour was free to go straight through in its turn.

Thus a prolonged and costly assault against a very heavily defended hill position was turned into a one night battle solely by infiltration tactics.

6. These methods are identical with those being employed on the Burma front to overcome Jap prepared positions. The phases of the operation in most cases follow the following lines :

(a) Patrolling to discover the extent of the position and the gaps in it.

(b) Infiltration through the gaps by sub-units and units.

(c) Establishment of " firm bases " in rear and on the flanks of the position to be attacked.

Thereafter the situation may develop in any or all of the following ways :

(i) The enemy may counter-attack from outside to try to relieve the beleaguered garrison.

(ii) The enemy may counter-attack from inside to try to escape or open his L of C.

(iii) The enemy may starve for lack of supplies.

(iv) The position may be attacked from any side, or from several sides at once.

7. A word about the consolidation of " firm bases ". With some difficulty, the idea of linear defence has been eliminated and that of all-round defence inculcated. But there are still some commanders who feel " naked " and anxious unless their line of approach is blocked and covered by fire. It is necessary to select the dominating tactical features which command the main lines of approach ; to hold them strongly all round and to keep reserves to blot out enemy infiltration parties. Experience has proved that a firm base may often best be established by a series of company positions (not smaller), each with its own reserves. These company positions may not always be able to support each other by fire. Each battalion and each brigade must hold reserves for attack against enemy infiltration, and all reserves must hasten to get to know their way about the country by day or night to fulfil their counter-infiltration tasks. It is impossible to prevent enemy infiltration, but the aim must always be to destroy the enemy parties which do get through BEFORE they have time to establish firm bases of their own.

8. Artillery can best be used in the infiltration attack for the following main tasks :

(a) Deception. By bringing down concentrations on located enemy positions from which he will infer attack from a direction which is actually NOT being made. Casualties to the enemy can also be increased by stopping concentrations for sufficiently long to enable him to come out of his holes and man his positions and then bringing them down again with a crash. Smoke can be used in conjunction with these concentrations to " put across " deception as to the line of attack.

(b) Cover by smoke. Infiltration must be invisible but open spaces have often to be crossed. Often, too, the way to the objective, once across the open, is so thick that it is too difficult to tackle by night. Again, we want to be able to vary the zero hours of attack and to use the unexpected times when the Jap is likely to be resting, eating, sleeping or foraging. This is the time to use smoke to cover our advance across the open or, possibly combined with concentrations, to deceive the Jap elsewhere.

(c) Support by observation When we have the enemy infiltrated, encircled, and, we hope, bewildered, we CANNOT *always afford to sit and starve him out. We will have to go in and mop him up.* Then will come the application of concentrated artillery fire by observation on enemy posts in turn. These concentrations should come from all available artillery within range and should be a real, good, hearty crack. If the targets have not already been registered, then very careful ranging will have to be carried out before such concentrations can be fired, owing to the proximity of our own troops.

(d) Defensive fire. The enemy counter-attack is a certainty. Infantry and artillery commanders must therefore settle on defensive fire tasks without delay to enable the maximum concentrations to be brought down when and where required.

9. **Air.**

(a) Bombers may be used on nodal points in the enemy's defended areas where we know that he is holding and must hold in strength. The attacks will continue till the targets have had a real "pasting". In this way we can ensure that the JAPS have been caused casualties and that some of their main positions which will eventually have to be mopped up have been "softened".

(b) Bombers and/or fighters may be employed against the enemy river and road communications to disorganise the moves of reserves and the maintenance of encircled garrisons with food and ammunition.

10. **Engineers.** Their main task will be to follow up our troops with tracks to enable their maintenance, first by mule, then by jeep. Pioneer platoons of battalions must help in this task. The point to be clear about is that the initial maintenance communications will generally have to follow an alignment different from the eventual main L of C. The forward tracks will in the first instance often have to be circuitous as they must be out of view of enemy operations and must follow the most secure route against enemy interference.

Assault engineer detachments will on occasion be required. These detachments should be earmarked, but should NOT be called up till their targets have been located. There will be plenty of time for this as the mopping up of defended areas which include bunkers will have to be deliberate.

11. Maintenance in ammunition, food and water, in that order of priority, must be assured for our troops behind the enemy by carrying forward as much as possible with them without hampering their tactical efficiency and by selecting and improving as rapidly as possible a reasonably secure maintenance route behind them. Carriers will sometimes be useful to get requirements forward over exposed areas. Escorts will have to be provided for mules if there is any danger of enemy interference. In some cases specific units, e. g., one platoon per company or one company per battalion may have to be detailed as porters for the initial maintenance of certain positions ; they should carry only rifles or TSMGs in addition to their load ; improvised bamboo stretchers are useful for the carriage of many loads. On some occasions it may be possible for maintenance to be effected by air.

2. SIX LESSONS FROM THE ARAKAN

The following are six important lessons learnt in the Arakan during February 1944. They are not new. They are mostly repetitions of facts which have been stated previously, but they must be emphasised and brought home to all concerned in the training of troops for warfare under jungle conditions.

1. Tactical Training.

Sufficient emphasis is not placed on minor tactics during training. This war is a platoon commanders' war and minor tactics are predominant. The Jap is cunning and must be met with cunning ; a head-on rush, though gallant, only results in unnecessary casualties. Junior leaders must realise that each little situation requires a plan and, when they make their plans, they must never forget deception, use of ground and fire.

2. Fire Discipline.

The standard of fire discipline is still far below requirements. There has been much indiscriminate firing, including firing at "noises". This is not only wasteful, but is exactly what the enemy wants. C. Os. and officers generally are not nearly strict enough in this respect and offenders should be punished.

Two rules to be observed are :—

(a) Do not fire until you see the yellow of the enemy's eyes.
(b) One round, one Jap.

3. Training of Administrative Units.

It is essential that all administrative units should undergo training in :—

(a) Fire discipline.	(c) Digging.	(e) Observation.
(b) Patrolling.	(d) Wiring.	(f) Fieldcraft.
		(g) Grenades.

4. Wire.

Commanders and troops are still not sufficiently wire-minded. They do not realise that wire must be placed out of enemy grenade range of our own positions. It can often best be used to block tracks, when dannert can be laid longways along the track so giving an obstacle in depth. It should be covered by fire, but many occasions will arise when this is not possible. Under these conditions it acts as a hindrance to the enemy, causes him to make a noise and gives warning of his approach.

5. Hygiene and Sanitation.

The standards of hygiene and sanitation amongst small units are often deplorable, and unless they are tightened up at once, fly-borne diseases will be excessive. Junior officers must realise that they are responsible for seeing that latrines are used by I. O. Rs., that waste food is burnt or buried and that the areas they occupy are clean. In some administrative units the I. O. Rs. have not had the same strict disciplinary training that exists in combatant units, but their standards of hygiene and sanitation must be the very highest.

6. Stand To.

Some units, particularly headquarters, are very bad in this respect. An officer or senior N. C. O. must be made responsible for going round at the appointed time to ensure that troops are standing to.

3. CUNNING, DECEPTION AND RUSES AS AN AID TO SURPRISE

1. The Japanese have proved themselves particularly susceptible and vulnerable to surprise, and from every front come accounts of how, when surprised, the enemy is liable either to panic or to carry out suicide attacks.

2. Every advantage must, therefore, be taken of this weakness in his armour, and new methods of cunning, new ruses and new means of deception must be continually sought and practised, in order to upset his balance and catch him "on the wrong leg".

3. The following paragraphs are included to stimulate ideas and imagination ; to get you thinking how you can fox the enemy, how you can make him do what YOU want, and how you can prevent him doing what he wants.

4. **Drawing His Fire** : Do we make enough use of noises to draw the enemy's fire ? There are only two ways of making certain that the enemy is on a position—by actually seeing him, or by drawing fire. Talking, coughing, digging, bamboo cutting are indications only. Till we get the proper apparatus for producing noises where we are NOT, patrols can easily produce "noises off" with a little ingenuity, e.g., sapper "bangs" with a fuse, bomb with a fuse, tin can on the end of a long string.

If you can simulate movement, it may also draw fire. Try a string tied to a bush to make it shake.

5. **Ambushes** : Our recce patrols often seem to bring in excellent information on which to base a successful ambush, e.g., normal movement of mules or MT along a road or track, a routine guard on a bridge, a phone wire behind an enemy post. All these afford good opportunities for ambushes. Patience, cunning, boldness and determination are required to bring off an ambush. Don't waste energy on laying ambushes where the odds are against the enemy turning up. A fairly certain method of ambushing is to cut a phone line and then lie up for the linesman or repair party. Remember that at night it is possible to perpetrate all sorts of nonsenses behind the enemy's lines and get away with it without difficulty. But instead of purely nuisance nonsense there should be good ambushes with bodies, papers and an occasional live specimen as a result.

Unless the enemy comes freely into the ambush where he may be trapped, the most carefully organised and set up ambush may be worthless. Therefore, reconnaissance of enemy trails, supply routes, etc., must be carried out carefully in order to determine the place where the ambush may be employed most successfully.

Suggested ambush locations are twisted trails, water points or "water holes", enemy defensive positions occupied only when the area defended is threatened (a favourite Jap tactic), supply routes used by carriers, and jungle stream trails. In any one of these locations it is often possible to ambush large enemy parties, patrols, or supply carriers.

Absolute concealment is essential in an ambush, as any suspicious appearance will put the enemy on his guard and surprise is lost. Movement, once the enemy becomes visible, is fatal, as you may be sure he will be keeping careful observation at all times.

The use of supporting riflemen concealed in trees must not be revealed by the scratching of bark or breaking of surrounding vines when the riflemen assume their position. Cigarette butts, paper scraps, ration tins, footprints and bruised or broken vegetation are positive indications to keen enemy eyes that all is not well.

The man in the ambush who must peer around the bush to see how far the enemy has entered the trap is the man who gives everything away and causes the death or injury of some of his companions. A good hunter must have patience, and in jungle fighting the soldier is a "hunter" in the strictest sense of the word.

An ambush needs depth. By depth is meant the distance which the enemy may penetrate into the ambush before his leading element passes out of the line of fire. This depth depends upon the size of the enemy party to be trapped and the number of trappers. When the enemy is fully in the position, there must be fire both in front and behind him to prevent his escape from either direction. The depth will depend, as well, upon the location of the ambush and its type.

It must be remembered that the principle of ambush is the annihilation of the entire enemy group, and depth must be governed accordingly.

Field of fire : It is seldom possible so to place weapons in an ambush as to make use of the optimum field of fire for each. No attempt should be made to place weapons in such a way as to maintain the so called correct range. Weapons should be brought closely into the ambush in order to bring point-blank fire to bear if possible ; the attendant roar adds to the confusion of the enemy, who more often than not give up the idea of escape as a result.

A successful ambush will probably cause an attempted enemy reprisal, especialy if one or more of the party escapes and can give accurate location of the ambush. Two courses are then open ; to ambush the reprisal in its turn, or to withdraw. If the first course is selected, particular care is necessary, as the enemy is likely to be on his guard and surprise will be especially difficult. In either case, consideration must be given to the easiest and swiftest means of withdrawal directly after the operation. This is of even greater importance if the ambush is behind enemy forward lines or in an enemy area, as it often is. If possible, two or three routes of withdrawal (none of which is the route of entry) should be reconnoitred carefully prior to going into position. Care must be taken in conducting this reconnaissance, as the enemy may well back-track and ambush your very route of withdrawal. Here again native scouts or guides should be used to cover tracks and search for the best routes.

Even the most careful preparation and planning of an ambush may be upset by an active and clever enemy ; and the tables may be turned with startling suddenness. When this takes place, groups or even individuals may find themselves cut off and forced to retire. If care has been taken to allot a R. V., and to make sure that all know its exact location, reorganisation may be effected and the tables turned on the enemy in such a way as to ead to his destruction.

VEREY LIGHT BOOBY ALARM

*T*HIS is an idea to disclose enemy patrols who may be investigating minefields at night. A number of Verey light cartridges are fixed to a piece of wood, cardboard or metal so that they stand rigidly upright. A length of FID (Fuse Instantaneous Detonating) such as cordtex or primacord is run under the board and tied so that it rests exactly beneath each cartridge detonating cap (Fig. 2). The board is buried so that the tops of the cartridges just stick above the ground.

A trip-wire, fixed between two posts or pegs, is attached to a pull-igniter, with detonator connected to the end of the FID (Fig. 3). When the wire is tripped, the Verey lights are automatically fired and, in brilliant light, disclose the enemy patrol (Fig. 1). Smart action on the trigger can mow them down at once.

This idea can be extended to employ other devices besides Verey lights, and can have a devastating effect on enemy morale.

(Designed by Major Fenton at METC)

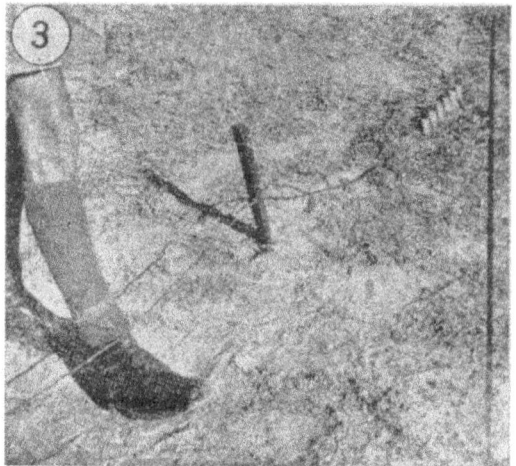

(To face page 9)

6. Booby Traps : A few in the enemy lines are worth trying, e. g., across a road or in one of the positions which he sometimes occupies. Consult the sappers and try a few. Let a sapper detachment go out on patrol with you to do the job and share in the fun and games.

Booby traps made with British 36 grenades are extremely simple in principle. Two variant forms are shown in sketches 1 and 3.

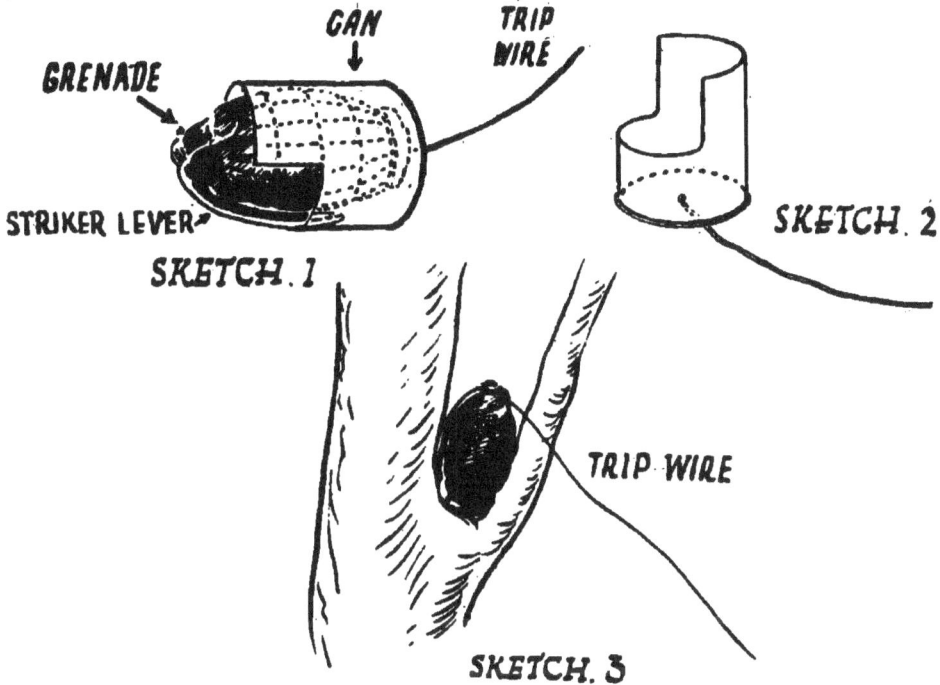

Sketch 1 is the "tinned" or "canned" variety, and sketch 3 the "tree fork" variety. Sketch 2 shows the way in which a tin can is cut so as to make it adaptable for use as a booby-trap mechanism. One end and a portion of a side of the can is cut away. A hole is put in the remaining end of the can through which the trip wire can be attached. The operation of the booby-trap is simplicity itself. The safety pin is removed, but the striker lever held down so that the grenade will not fire. The grenade is then inserted into the cut out tin can so that the striker lever is held inside the remaining circular portion of the can. The grenade and tin can are held together and placed on the ground. In this position the grenade is safe until the trip wire is disturbed. When a pull is exerted on the trip wire, the tin can is pulled away from the grenade. The grenade being relatively heavy remains in place. The lever is released, and the grenade detonates. Another form of the tin can method is to place the grenade in the can in the same way and to balance the can on a limb. When pressure is exerted on the trip wire, the can falls over ; the grenade drops out, the lever is released, and the grenade detonates. The tree fork variation is worked on the same principle. The space between limbs serves the same function as the can. When the trip wire is disturbed the grenade falls out of the tree and explodes.

The trip wires can be strung loose in the heavy undergrowth and attached to long vines and creepers. In dense jungle they are difficult to detect. As the attackers move through the heavy undergrowth, a pull here or there on a creeper explodes a grenade. Casualties from these simple and effective devices are heavy.

Booby-traps are neutralised by grasping the grenade firmly holding the striker lever down and inserting a small nail in the safety pin hole.

Note also the Verey light booby alarm illustrated opposite page 9.

7. **Bomb Alleys :** A useful way of putting bombs where you want them, i. e., when the enemy is heard to have reached a certain point below your post, is to have bomb alleys cut through the jungle with a stop at the end where you want the explosion to take place.

8. **Protection against Grenades :** There have been a number of casualties from JAP grenades landing in our trenches. It is quite a good idea to build a bamboo grill in front of your slit trench or foxhole which is so designed as NOT to interfere with your own fire or action but to explode the enemy's percussion bomb, which is really only danger-ous if it actually hits you or bursts within a foot or so of you.

Similarly, when in position on the slope of a hill, it is a good plan to dig another trench behind your weapon pit so that grenades which strike the ground above the weapon will roll into this trench and explode harmlessly. See illustration below :

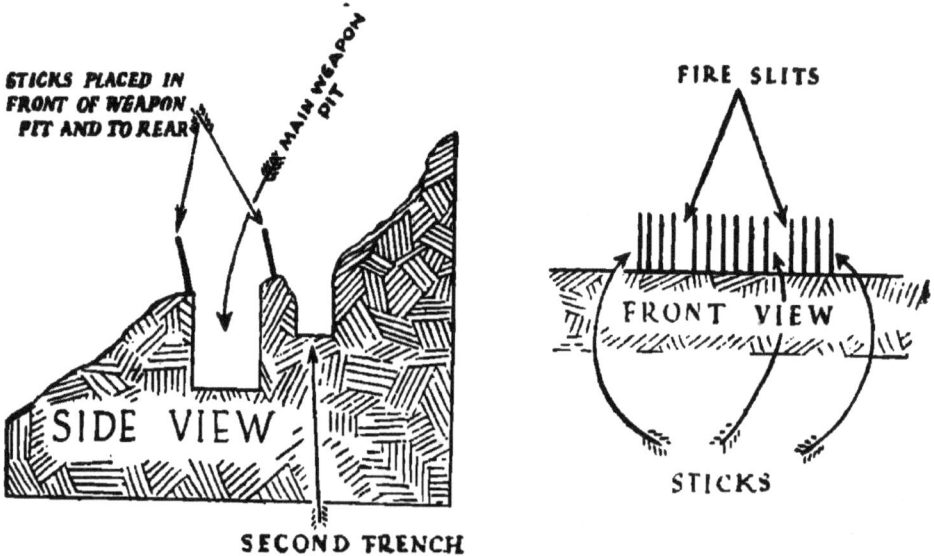

STICKS PLACED IN FRONT OF WEAPON PIT AND TO REAR

MAIN WEAPON PIT

SIDE VIEW

SECOND TRENCH

FIRE SLITS

FRONT VIEW

STICKS

Note : The sticks must be camouflaged.

9. **Concealing Your Route :** On entering a village, ask questions about the places you are NOT INTERESTED in as well as those in which you are. If you take a guide, then, if possible, avoid telling him where you are going till you are well clear of the village.

As an example of how to mislead the enemy, imagine three villages. A, B and C ;

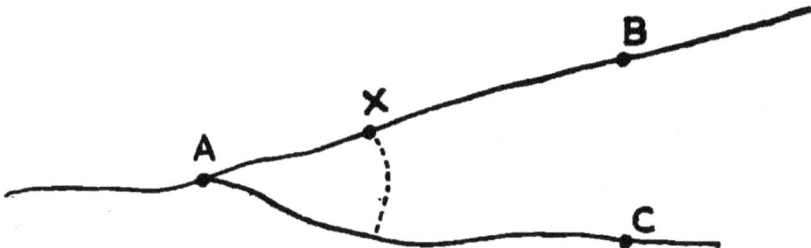

You wish to move your platoon from A to B. Go into the village at A and ask for a guide. Go far enough down the road towards C to make sure that the guide is certain that the party is going that way. Then tip him and send him home. Once the guide is well out of sight of the rearmost soldiers, the platoon splits up into sections who make their way to an R. V. at X. The platoon having assembled at X, move to B.

Remember, whatever the size of the force, it MUST split up to go to the R. V. as any party bigger than a section leaves too obvious a track, or otherwise draws attention.

Another way of preventing the enemy from knowing which way a party has gone is to march down a chaung (river), in shallow water. The whole party MUST NOT leave the chaung in one body, but singly and in different places, because single tracks are less noticeable.

Remember that the boots worn by the Japanese troops are very different from those worn by us. If patrols occasionally take off their boots, their bare foot-prints will NOT be distinguishable from those of the locals. The enemy often do this.

10. **Concealing Your Strength :** Quite often it may be necessary to give the enemy an exaggerated idea of the strength of a column moving through the jungle, in order to hide our actual weakness from him.

One way of getting this information over to the Japs is as follows:

Suppose the complete force to be 250 strong. A village is entered and the headman ordered to produce enough supplies for 500 men. The food is produced and half of it eaten, and the balance is then taken off into the jungle for the other imaginary 250 to eat. This ruse has been practised by both sides with success in the CHINDWIN and KABAW valleys.

11. **Distracting the Enemy's Attention from the Direction of the Assault :** Every plan must consist of deception to draw the enemy's fire and attention, while a determined assault party gets in and does the killing.

Deception can be attained by battle cries, drawing bamboo bundles on long pieces of vine through the jungle, and the occasional shot. It should aim at drawing fire on the easier lines of approach. If there is wire with booby traps attached these might be detonated in the required directions by throwing a long string or vine with a weight on the end and pulling from a covered position.

The actual assault should be carried out by a small but determined party with bombs and rifles or tommy-guns. Often the best line of approach for the assault party will be over the steepest and most difficult ground because defilade from automatic fire can then often be obtained ; also obstacles and booby traps are unlikely to be on that side and attack from that direction will be unexpected.

As soon as the assault party gets in, the rest of the attackers must advance, complete mopping up and consolidate.

DECEPTION IS A WEAPON

"All warfare is based on deception. Hence, when able to attack, we must seem unable to do so ; when using our forces, we must seem inactive ; when we are near, we must make the enemy believe we are far away, and when far, we must make him think we are near. Hold out baits to entice him. Feign disorder, and crush him. If he is superior in strength, evade him. If he is taking his ease, give him no rest. If his forces are united, separate them. Attack him where he is unprepared, appear where you are not expected. These military devices, leading to victory, must not be divulged beforehand."

Sun Tzu in "The Art of War", about 500 B. C.

4. SNIPERS AND SNIPING

1. The Enemy Sniper.

In all operations, both offensive and defensive, the use of snipers by Japanese forces is well known. The term "sniper", when applied to the Japanese, is usually misused. The average Jap sniper is a mere rifleman who has obtained for himself an advantageous position such as a tree-top from which to fire at his enemy. The true Jap sniper, skilfully camouflaged, supplied with concentrated rations and specially armed, is responsible for only a small amount of what is so often termed "sniper fire".

The nuisance and morale value of sniper fire is being continually illustrated on all fronts. Snipers present a constant problem in both front line and rear areas. On some occasions it has been found necessary to employ patrols with the sole task of eliminating Jap snipers who had infiltrated into our lines. There is nothing more disconcerting than to have a battalion, or even a regimental command post, line of supply, or communications, subjected to sporadic fire from a source unknown. Although, in most cases, this fire is extremely inaccurate and causes few casualties, the psychological factor involved is important.

2. Neutralizing the Enemy Sniper.

Along jungle tracks Jap snipers will seldom fire at parties larger than three or more, because they fear detection by the remainder of the group. Similarly, groups of two or three men searching for snipers by maintaining careful watch or by active patrolling, have a similar deterrent effect. Therefore individuals should never travel alone in rear areas where sniper fire may be encountered. Three men are better than two. The alertness of sentries and sub-units of H. Q. defence units will do much towards acting as a deterrent to the Jap sniper.

One method that has worked in the detection of snipers on several occasions is worth noting here. When a member of patrol is struck by sniper fire, careful determination of the position and attitude of the victim when he was struck and a back bearing taken along the direction of the wound, may often expose the approximate area from which the shot was fired. A careful search of this area will often lead to the discovery of the sniper.

3. Employment of Our Own Snipers.

It is useless employing a sniper who is not a very good shot and field-craftsman. It is essential that the sniper is not used in a happy-go-lucky and "what can we give him to do" manner. There must be a clearcut object in his operations and this must be explained to him and his mate (they should always work in pairs), so that a correct selection of targets can be made.

Normally their targets will be of four types dependent on the object :

    (a) To kill officers, N. C. Os. and Signal personnel in order to destroy control.

    (b) To kill the crews of L. M. Gs., M. M. Gs. and mortars in order to destroy the enemy fire power.

    (c) To kill individuals moving along the L of C to compel the enemy to move in larger numbers and thereby weaken his strength on his main front.

    (d) To kill Japs indiscriminately to lower the general enemy morale

Selection of Positions.

The greatest care is necessary in the selection and preparation of the sniper's lair. Get above your enemy where you can. Having selected the position, choose an alternative, and when you move to that, choose another. Prepare the position at first or last light and get into it in the dark, being careful to leave no tracks.

5. Concealment.

Use natural rather than cut vegetation. The latter will wither quickly. If you must cut vegetation, use evergreens and palms, as they last longer.

Watch the sunlight and shadow and don't forget that the latter moves. Remember to break your outline, both head and body, and merge it into the background, but remember that as the day goes on, the light, shade and colour of that background may change.

6. Patience.

For the sniper, unlimited patience is the most important attribute after marksmanship. You must be prepared to sit or lie motionless for long periods. Don't be hurried over your shooting but be certain of your shot. The Jap you refrain from shooting today, because it was an odds-against shot, will turn up again and give you a better shot to-morrow or the next day because he hasn't been scared. The old R. S. M.'s slogan, "Wait for it! Wait for it!" is a good one for the sniper. The most difficult time to obey it is at dusk when the light is going and you haven't had a shot all day.

7. Guile.

Don't forget that your concealment and, therefore, your un-interrupted killing of Japs is dependent on your ability to go on foxing him as to where you are.

The Jap trick of a string to a neighbouring tree is a good one. Better still, make something move on a different level to yourself in relation to your target. For example, if you are on the ground on a forward slope, shake a bush on the sky line or, if you are up a tree move a bush on ground level.

If you have fired several shots on one day from one hide, the next day shoot from your alternative position.

Remember that a sudden noise will often cause your target to stop, look and listen, and so give you a sitting shot instead of a moving one.

What would you do if you suddenly saw a bit of white stuff waving on a stick? If you were not very wary, you would probably keep your eye on that bit of white stuff and cautiously approach it. What cold meat you would be for a sniper concealed to a flank! Try it on the Jap. All you want is a bit of rag, a bit of bamboo and a bit of string, but watch out that the Jap does not have to pass your string when approaching your bait.

5. JUNGLE OPERATION INSTRUCTIONS

(RECEIVED FROM A DIVISION IN THE PACIFIC THEATRE)

Action of Individuals.

No lights of any kind will be used in forward positions during hours of darkness and **No Smoking** unless specifically authorised by higher headquarters.

Silence is essential at the front and on patrol. If the enemy can't locate you, every advantage is with you. He will try by every means to get you to disclose your position so that he can gain the advantage over you.

Don't shoot unless you have something worth-while to shoot at. Blind shooting simply gives away your location and may kill your own comrades.

Be on guard for all types of booby traps and other enemy ruses.

Japanese light mortar fire is accurate; therefore, grouping of personnel must be strictly avoided, and individuals will not allow themselves to be silhouetted on the skyline.

Dig in whenever halted and improve holes as time permits.

Talk only in as low a tone as possible. Practise whispering especially in telephone conversations. Use signals, such as hand or arm signals, tapping on the rifle, bird calls, etc., as much as possible. Do not expose yourself any more than necessary when using hand or arm signals. Remember the careless soldier, who unnecessarily exposes himself, jeopardises the security and lives of his team mates.

Be on the lookout for false surrender; any offer of surrender must be suspected as an enemy ruse.

Do not use field-glasses openly: observe the same principles as in firing the rifle from concealment.

Do not forget that many Japanese speak English. At night a favourite trick is for them to infiltrate and yell false orders such as "Withdraw", or "Sergeant, where are you?" Learn to know the voice of your leader. Japanese have difficulty in pronouncing the letter "l".

Do not attempt to retrieve enemy wounded. (It may be a trick).

Do not forget to look up before you move. Get into the habit of watching tops of trees as well as their roots.

Remember, this war with the Japanese is a war of KILL or GET KILLED. You are a **better man, better armed** and a **superior marksman**.

Do not permit straggling, and do not straggle yourself.

Rumours are a curse ; don't start them or . believe them, and wait for verification.

Do not try to win the war single-handed. Use team work, live and be successful.

Learn the difference between a hero and a fool. The former has commonsense as well as courage.

Remember, there are no wet nurses in action.

When fired on by snipers, move at top speed to the nearest cover or concealment. As soon as possible, quietly change your location, then locate and destroy the sniper. Do not, under any circumstances, stand still in the open.

Basic Measures to Counter Jap Tactics.

Every effort will be made to capture Jap prisoners. Send them at once under guard to the rear. They are the source of valuable information.

It is imperative for morale that all officers maintain a cheerful and optimistic attitude, and that they do not show by word or action any discouragement or evidence of fatigue. All officers must exhibit a desire for aggressive offensive combat, and instill the same desire in their men.

Each platoon commander, or other small unit leader, will take every opportunity to instruct, talk over, discuss, and re-discuss with his men, Japanese tactics, and our methods of operating against them, and work out in detail the methods his unit will employ to get team work in their day and night operations against the enemy. It is essential that officers and men know and understand each other thoroughly.

Patrolling.

Specially trained scouts should be used by each company. Laying of ambushes on trails or near water holes has been an excellent method of harassing the Japanese and reducing their numbers.

Jungle Operations.

Push forward trails for vehicles for carrying supplies as far as possible. Native carriers will be used to the maximum extent available. Even so, experience indicates that about one-fifth of the fighting force of each battalion may have to be employed as carrying parties and to maintain the supply of ammunition, food, and water, and to handle the evacuation of casualties. This number should be kept at the minimum, and as soon as carrying parties are no longer needed they must be returned to the front.

Night Operations.

The Japanese usually have their main attack directed at a flank. This is accompanied by a display of noise to our front. Under cover of this noise an advanced echelon of men, carrying grenades, creeps or crawls quietly up to our lines. Their mission is to throw grenades at our automatic weapons if we open fire prematurely at the noise created by the main body of demonstration forces. Therefore, **NEVER, REPEAT NEVER, OPEN FIRE AT NIGHT AT A NOISE.**

Limit movement at night to the absolute minimum.

Cover luminous watches or other objects that will shine at night.

For identification, use the prescribed password. When challenging or replying to a challenge, **speak quietly.** Remember, the enemy also has ears.

Individuals, or units, that are lost when night falls should select a covered position and remain for the night.

Individual Equipment.

Care of equipment will be strictly enforced. Do not let men get separated from their equipment. Unit leaders must require daily care of equipment.

Darken any equipment to make it blend with tropical green, and dull items that might glisten or reflect light.

Watchfulness.

Our troops need training in remaining quiet and motionless for long periods.

Commanders should never be addressed by rank when in contact with enemy troops. It is a sure way to lose officers. The same applies to NCOs.

When challenging at night the sentry should remain concealed. Never permit an unknown person to come within knife range.

---

6. OPERATIONAL NOTES FROM ITALY

The Country.

Tanks got to some surprising places, and often failed in what appeared to be easy places, so it was very difficult to say whether tanks could do a certain job or not, but it is always worth a try. The value of tanks in unexpected places is incalculable : e.g. at R. LI. COLLE there were mines, but not a single anti-tank gun, and only a few tanks were enough to wring the cry from a German officer, "Tanks in my position—I am destroying my wireless—God Save Germany !"

Co-operation.

It is remarkable what can be achieved by troops who know each other and have mutual confidence. For one attack, the tanks and infantry had ample opportunity to discuss the plan, and in point of fact lived together for some time. Consequently, although the show did not go entirely according to plan, no mistakes were made, neither party blamed the other, and both got down to it and worked together to ensure the complete success that they achieved.

Intercommunication.

The old bugbear of intercommunication between infantry and tanks was met. At times infantry and tanks had to approach from different directions, and on such occasions the infantry must seek out the tanks—they can hear their engines and spot them through the trees much more quickly than the tanks can see the infantry. It is entirely wrong that tank officers should have to go hunting about on their feet to contact the infantry. The mounting of 38 sets in certain tanks successfully provided direct communication between tanks and infantry on several occasions.

Tanks in Battle.

Every single man must be 100% alert all the time and may be called upon to use his initiative and intelligence at any moment. One tank may find itself quite alone and unable to see any other tank. Quick and accurate shooting is perhaps the only essential factor that can be actually taught—the remainder requires quick appreciation, quick decision, quick action and the ability to deal with situations not catered for in any training manual. Drivers need to be of the very highest class. In soft ground, tanks must not "track" one another and if drivers can be taught, when it is necessary to follow in line ahead, to drive two or three feet right or left of the tank in front, a lane is soon made where large numbers can pass. Gear selection too is of vital importance, so as to avoid changing down, which means halting in bad places. In this type of country there is more temptation than elsewhere for crews to abandon their tanks as soon as anything goes wrong. A tank on a mine is a most valuable pillbox and it must be drummed in to all ranks that they must never abandon a tank without orders unless the tank is on fire, likely to fall into enemy hands, or its guns are out of action.

7. THE CROSSING OF THE VOLTURNO

AN ACCOUNT.

Topography.

The VOLTURNO is not a wide river, but it is remarkable for the height and sheer nature of its banks. They vary from 15 to some 35 or even 40 feet and are perpendicular.

NORTH of the VOLTURNO the ground rises abruptly after some 8 miles into steep hills and mountains. The country is very close and movement off the road was always difficult and often impossible for any vehicle.

In one sector there were 43 "blows" (bridges or craters) in $2\frac{1}{2}$ miles, and it took 4 days to move forward 3 miles despite superhuman efforts by sappers. Heavy rain which damaged bridges and rendered diversions useless added to the difficulties.

Deception was carried out and surprise eventually achieved by recce and heavy artillery fire being carried out all along the front. As a result, the enemy did not know when or where the attacks were coming, and revealed his defensive fire tasks.

Careful reconnaissance, patrolling, the need for rehearsal and training in boating etc. and fool-proof plans for getting anti-tank guns across were the main lessons of the operation.

1. German Method of Holding the River Line.

Generally speaking the actual banks of the VOLTURNO were not heavily mined.

In the village of CONCELLO, where one crossing was made, mines were laid under the flagstones of the road. These presented considerable difficulty. They were often placed in pairs with a charge and press igniter on top. This was covered with loose earth and the flagstones were then replaced. The results were, firstly, that the detector would not pick up the mines through the flagstones, whilst the latter which often have a metal content caused unnecessary digging. Secondly, the mines only go off after a number of vehicles have gone over them and compressed the earth.

The enemy held the NORTH bank of the VOLTURNO and patrolled the SOUTH bank. He had fixed lines of fire along the banks and on the railway bridge. His tanks were held back some 2000 yards in a counter-attack role.

2. The Reconnaissance of the River Line.

Reconnaissance of the river line by day was out of the question.

Several points came out of the consequent reconnaissance patrolling at night. Most of them are not new.

(a) The same unit that is to make the crossing must do the reconnaissance. It is tempting to avoid this as it is a big strain, but it must be done.

(b) The study of air photos is most important. Maps in this case were useless.

(c) The briefing of the patrol must be very detailed. It must include an R.E. representative, and some essential questions are :

    (i) Is the river suitable for rafting ?

    (ii) What time will be required to make the raft and prepare the bank on the other side ?

    (iii) Are the approaches on both sides suitable ?

    (iv) What type of river bed is it ?

(d) Patrols were up to a platoon in strength, but the greater part of these big patrols was used to cover those actually crossing the river.

3. Notes on Roles of Infantry and Royal Engineers.

In this formation the Pioneers did the greater part of the mine clearance leaving the Royal Engineers to tackle the rafting. A definite preference for the Pioneers to tackle the mines was expressed by more than one C.O.

4. Organization of the Crossing.

The diagrams on page 19 are not to scale.

(i) (a) Anti-tank defence on far side must not rely on rafts. Anti-tank platoons must start to get guns across by improvised means as soon as companies are established on the far bank. Guns may be taken to pieces or winched.

    (b) If anti-tank guns are not in position by first light they probably will not get there at all.

    (c) Some vehicle to tow anti-tank guns away from the far bank if rafting fails is very desirable. The amphibious jeep may be the only answer.

(a) Before the Crossing.

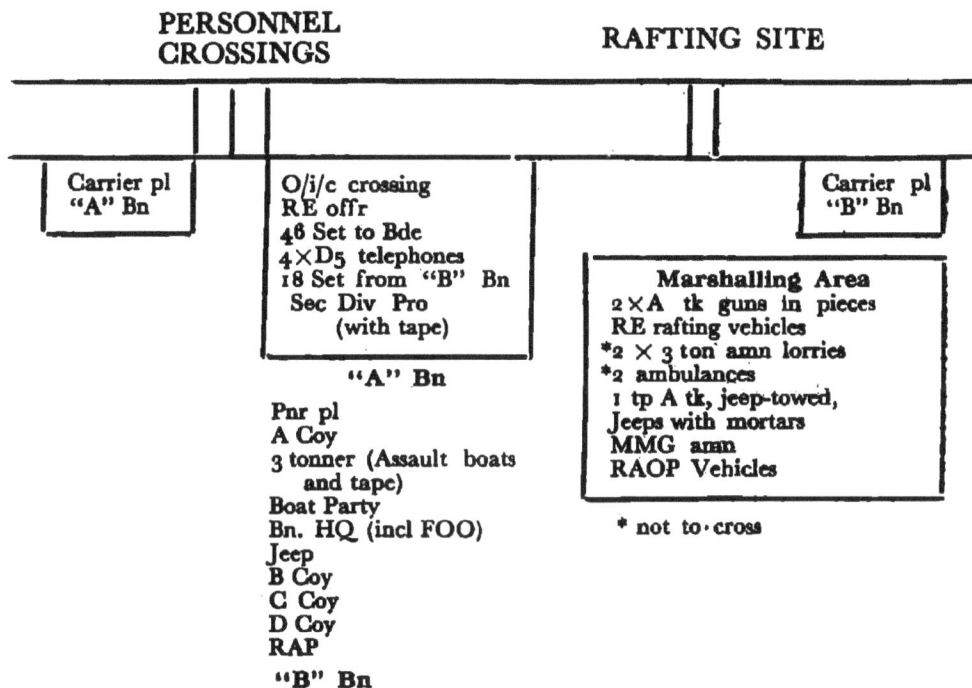

PERSONNEL CROSSINGS

RAFTING SITE

Carrier pl "A" Bn

O/i/c crossing
RE offr
46 Set to Bde
4×D5 telephones
18 Set from "B" Bn
Sec Div Pro
(with tape)

Carrier pl "B" Bn

Marshalling Area
2×A tk guns in pieces
RE rafting vehicles
*2 × 3 ton amn lorries
*2 ambulances
1 tp A tk, jeep-towed,
Jeeps with mortars
MMG amn
RAOP Vehicles

* not to·cross

"A" Bn

Pnr pl
A Coy
3 tonner (Assault boats and tape)
Boat Party
Bn. HQ (incl FOO)
Jeep
B Coy
C Coy
D Coy
RAP

"B" Bn

(b) After Initial Surprise Lost

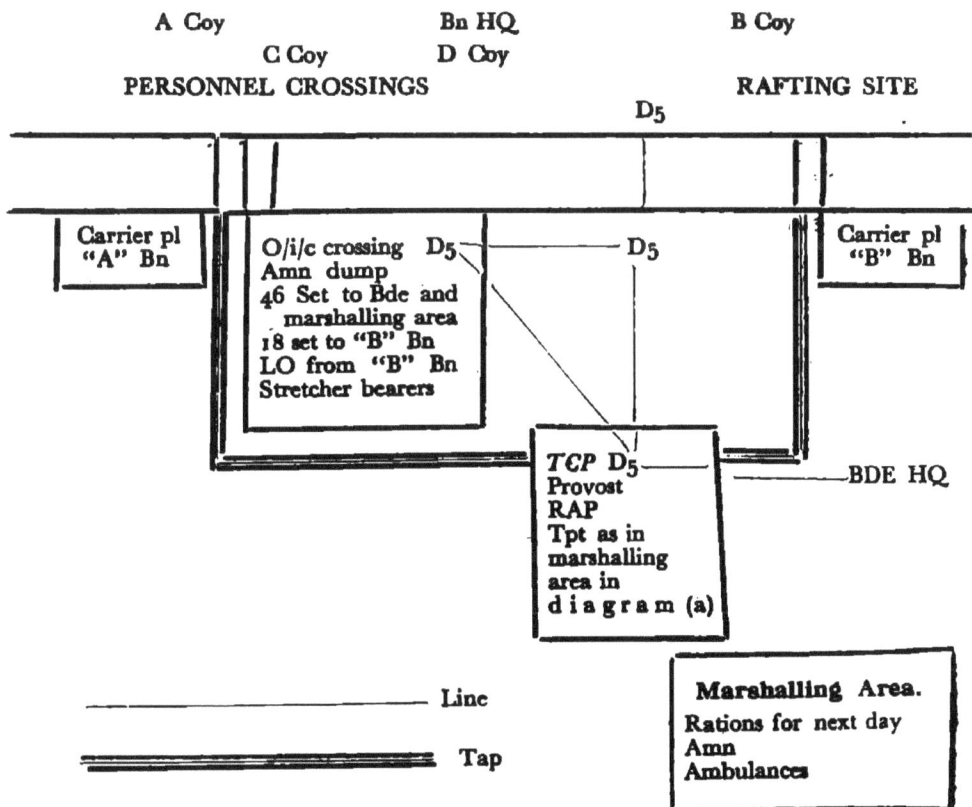

A Coy   Bn HQ   B Coy
C Coy   D Coy
PERSONNEL CROSSINGS   RAFTING SITE
D5

Carrier pl "A" Bn

O/i/c crossing   D5
Amn dump
46 Set to Bde and marshalling area
18 set to "B" Bn
LO from "B" Bn
Stretcher bearers

D5

Carrier pl "B" Bn

TCP D5
Provost
RAP
Tpt as in marshalling area in diagram (a)

BDE HQ

————— Line

═════ Tap

Marshalling Area.
Rations for next day
Amn
Ambulances

(ii) (a) Several personnel crossings with rope should be made.

   (b) Every effort must be made to find wading crossings. Much time is lost in boating.

(iii) (a) The traffic control post should not be on a X road or other obvious DF task.

   (b) The TCP should have adjoining cover for daylight.

(iv) (a) Wheeled and tracked vehicles should not approach by the same track.

   (b) All tracks must be clearly marked early.

5. Notes on Requirements in Artillery Support.

The artillery was used to cover the crossing. The approach was silent and the artillery was used as part of a deception plan, i.e., shooting where the attack was not coming. Once across, DF tasks came into play and of course an FOO went over early. Traces from air photos with DF tasks covering the front were issued down to platoon commanders.

6. Defence and Extension of the Bridgehead.

The defence of the bridgehead depended on getting the anti-tank guns across. One crossing eventually failed because the guns did not get across. Insurance in this matter is essential, and some guns taken over in pieces so as not to rely on the rafting is recommended.

7. Policy and Scope for Use of Tanks.

Tanks and pheasants were landed on the NORTH bank from the sea. They met difficulties with mines but eventually some got up and at least held off the Boche tanks. The writer thought that they might have been used to extend the bridgehead in certain places. They were not so used to any great extent.

8. General Notes :

(a) It is quicker and better to wade than to boat. The leading pioneer platoon tests for a wading place and gets the rope across. There should be 3 ropes at 3 different places. The present toggle rope is too heavy. A light ¼" is required. The absence of rope on the far bank which was high and steep caused a traffic block and delay of 1 hour.

(b) Specially trained boat carriers are very important. There was little or no opportunity for any rehearsal or special training before the attack. EVERY MINUTE SPENT ON REHEARSAL PAYS A BIG DIVIDEND.

(c) The anti-tank platoon, pioneers and spare drivers seem the most suitable to be given boat training. Rifle companies cannot spare the men. Stretcher bearers should be trained in dealing with a stretcher on an assault boat.

(d) Crossing a river takes a long time. Plans were far too optimistic. It is impossible to lay down a time for general guidance, but roughly, one leading battalion took 2 hours. The second battalion waded across in 1 hour.

8. OPERATIONS IN ITALY: ADMINISTRATION

(TAKEN FROM 8 INDIAN DIVISION TRAINING INSTRUCTION)

THE BACKGROUND.

(a) During the period under review the division advanced a distance of approximately 55 miles. Except for the actual build-up and forcing of the SANGRO crossing, the division advanced on its own axis.

(b) The advance was over the lower slopes of the Appenines across the grain of the country which consisted of steep ridges of cultivated hills, varying in height from 800 to 3,000 feet above sea level. The country is intersected by three main valleys, those of the rivers BIFERNO, TRIGNO and SANGRO.

(c) The division axis and maintenance route was with few exceptions a single second class hill road, generally passable for two way traffic but with many bottle necks and bridges, the latter almost without exception destroyed by enemy action necessitating the erection of Bailey bridging or the construction of one way diversions.

(d) The weather was a major factor in administrative planning, four days wet being usually followed by an equivalent period with little or no rain. During periods of heavy rain the roads were extremely slippery and the state of the ground and tracks off the roads was such that vehicles easily became bogged.

(e) Enemy tactics aimed to impose the maximum delay on our advance relying largely on the weather and demolitions to achieve this end. At the two major obstacles of the rivers TRIGNO and SANGRO a firm stand was made.

THE ADMINISTRATIVE PROBLEM.

The problem was to ensure that despite long and often unreliable communications, administrative needs were always ready at hand for the forward troops during the advance and that resources were sufficient or were readily procurable to allow of a build-up for a major action. If it became apparent that the rate of the advance would at any time outstrip in the available resources for supply and maintenance, then attention would have to be called to this fact.

THE LESSONS.

(a) General.

All administrative resources with few exceptions were kept under division control, administrative units and installations being leap-frogged through each other to keep pace with the advance. This system worked well; it ensured that one leg was always on the ground and that a reserve for unforeseen eventualities was available. The disadvantage that administrative units did not always work exclusively with their affiliated brigades was outweighed by the advantages gained. A principle rigidly adhered to was to place sufficient administrative resources across an obstacle at the earliest opportunity so that if communications broke, troops across that obstacle could continue fighting.

(b) Supply.

(i) The system of having a division maintenance area (D.M.A.) in which is located ammunition, supply and petrol points was adopted and worked satisfactorily. During the advance on a single road on which a system of block traffic timings is often necessary it was found that, in order to ensure that replenishment by units was not delayed, two such maintenance areas were normally required. The forward division maintenance area (F.D.M.A.) maintaining the forward units and drawing its supplies through the rear D.M.A. which in turn drew from the F.M.C. As the advance progressed the F.D.M.A. became the rear D.M.A. and a fresh F.D.M.A. was moved forward. If two D.M.As. were not necessary a nucleus for forming a F.D.M.A. was always kept available at short notice ready to push forward when occasion demanded. In addition it was sometimes necessary to form a forward ammunition point for ammunition other than gun ammunition so that this was within easy reach of forward troops. The above system ensured that troops were at all times within comparatively easy reach of their supplies and that when communications broke owing to weather or enemy action a reserve of supplies was available near at hand.

(ii) A reserve of supplies varying from three to five days with a corresponding reserve of ammunition and POL was always carried by forward troops ; this is necessary to cover the period when forward troops find themselves on the far side of an obstacle before it has been possible to establish a F.D.M.A. over it. A case in point was the crossing of the SANGRO when it was only possible in the initial stages to establish a forward ammunition point over the river. All units crossing had been ordered to carry five days' rations, one first and one second line reserve of ammunition and estimated requirements for three days' POL for the limited number of vehicles they took over with them, at the same time whenever possible daily maintenance was carried on by mules and light vehicles. These measures proved satisfactory in keeping all troops across the river fully maintained until such time as the bridging situation admitted of establishing a F.D.M.A. on the far bank and of a reversion to the normal system of maintenance.

(iii) When supply on a pack basis had to be resorted to "compo" rations proved valuable owing to ease of loading and distribution, this form of ration is very popular with British troops owing to the variety of the ingredients provided for them. Indian troops as a whole prefer the normal ration. Cigarettes should not be included in the Indian "compo" rations. The normal ration has proved good and supplies adequate with the exception of meat on hoof—the chief difficulty appears to be that the autumn is the breeding season for a large number of Italian sheep and goats.

(c) Transport.

(i) **First Line M. T.** When operating over narrow roads in hilly country it has been found that in order to speed up movement generally, M. T. in forward areas must be reduced to a minimum. To achieve this units have been placed on a reduced scale of first line M. T., the balance being formed into a divisional vehicle pool located in a back area. This pool forms a useful reserve of transport from which to make immediate replacements to units and to meet small unforeseen and urgent demands or transport in rear areas.

(ii) **Second Line M. T.** Lengthy and uncertain communications, often necessitate a 48-hour turn round for vehicles. Owing to this and many varying commitments such as ammunition dumping, troop carrying and moves of stores and supplies during the advance, all of which are liable to be required at short notice, it has been found necessary to keep all M.T. resources under divisional control. The allotment of this transport is made by HQ Division R. I. A. S. C. on orders issued by Q Staff.

(iii) **Pack Transport.** One and a half Indian pack transport companies and one field ambulance troop have been under command of the division for the operations. Total strength approximately 500 load carrying mules and 24 casualty carrying mules. This form of transport has been invaluable and of the greatest use when improvisation has been necessary to cross obstacles.

Pack transport has been used for both first and second line work to cross obstacles which vehicles could not negotiate. On one occasion a troop of tanks behind whom the road broke were supplied on mule transport for three days. The most economical method of using pack transport resources has been found to be to establish a mule camp in proximity to the D.M.A. and for divisional Q Staff to allot mules for first or second line work on an "as required" basis.

(d) Medical.

(i) It has been found desirable to keep one company of its affiliated field ambulance permanently under command of each infantry brigade. The HQ and remaining company being kept under divisional control for employment as the situation demands. The company under brigade command can on occasion be allotted sufficient mules to form an A.D.S. carried on a pack basis.

(ii) When pushing medical installations across an obstacle, a light M.D.S. with a field surgical unit attached has been found valuable. Such an M.D.S. was moved across the river on a pack basis in the early stages of the SANGRO battle.

(ii) Evacuation over difficult country from forward areas has called for improvisation. Ordinary ambulance cars cannot normally operate under such conditions though the light Humber 4 wheel drive ambulance has been of the greatest value. Evacuation by mule has been much used, litters being found a much better form of transport than cacholets. Many jeeps in the division have been converted to stretcher carrying and it is hoped eventually to have all jeeps so equipped. The necessary equipment is made in divisional workshops and is easily removable—it allows of two stretcher cases being carried, and does not prejudice the use of the vehicle for its normal functions.

(e) Repair and Recovery.

(i) In order that brigades shall have immediately at hand light repair and recovery facilities, advanced sections of brigade workshop companies have been left under brigade command. The HQ and rear section of brigade workshop companies have been kept under divisional control and leap-frogged forward in turn as the advance progresses. In order to allow of workshops functioning to capacity it is essential that once they are established workshops should be moved as seldom as possible.

(ii) On narrow roads with heavy traffic it is essential that recovery to the rear is not permitted during the move forward of the division. Damaged vehicles must be removed from the road to avoid traffic blocks and left there until it is possible to move repair organisations forward to deal with them when traffic clears.

(iii) With the exception of the recovery vehicles of advance sections of workshops under brigade control it has been found necessary to keep all remaining recovery vehicles under divisional control operated by the CIEME and located during the advance at bad bottle necks or diversions. Although heavy recovery vehicles are allowed on the establishment of an Indian Division none heavier than six wheeled 3 ton have as yet been supplied and it has been necessary to rely on loans from higher formations to make good this deficiency. Such vehicles are essential for use on diversions in bad weather.

(f) Ordnance.

(i) In order to ensure speedy issues of ordnance spares it has been found advisable to locate brigade sections of the divisional ordnance field park with B echelons of the brigades concerned—the HQ section being located in reasonable proximity to RAB echelon.

(g) Provost and Traffic Control.

With indifferent communications, when traffic blocks can seriously affect the rate of advance of the division, it is essential that all provost resources are kept under divisional control so that allotments can be made according to the situation as it changes. The following points are worth noting :—

    (i) Ample and early sign posting especially for traffic circuits and through town and villages.

    (ii) Provost to work in close co-operation with RE and IEME regarding traffic control on diversions and bad bottlenecks.

    (iii) The allocation of small detachments from the provost company for permanent duty at the D. M. A. where traffic is at times very heavy. In order to avoid traffic congestion the D.M.A. should whenever possible be sited off the main axis, and ammunition supply and petrol points be kept well apart.

    (iv) The need for the provision of at least six telephones and six miles of cable to the provost company to enable them to operate difficult one way stretches of road.

Unless operations are to be prejudiced the divisional provost company must be composed of selected personnel who are 100% proficient and units must also have a proportion of their personnel trained in traffic duties so that they can take on traffic control in their own areas.

(h) Organisation Divisional HQ (A/Q Branch).

(i) In order that Q may be continually in the picture and ready to implement the commander's plan without delay it has been found that the most efficient organisation for A/Q branch in the field is for the A/Q and D/Q to have a "Q" operations office at main divisional headquarters. At rear divisional HQ are located the D/A and staff captain with the services. Divisional HQ is only split when necessary but with an advance on a narrow front this is often unavoidable. On such occasions rear division besides fulfilling its normal function of relieving "Q" operations of routine work carries out a useful role in controlling under orders of main A/Q the move forward of rear units with which it is in close touch.

(ii) It has been found advisable for the ADMS normally to live at main divisional HQ so that he is in close touch with the forward situation; other heads of services visit main divisional HQ as necessary. All services officers are located at rear divisional HQ.

(j) Administrative Command.

(i) An independent administrative R/T link has proved essential. Wireless sets available allow only of communication between main and rear HQ staff captains of brigades, and the D.M.A. If additional sets were available such communication would also be established to the M.D.S. and the second D.M.A. or forward ammunition points if formed.

(ii) A small R/T link from CIEME at divisional HQ to important recovery points would be of very great assistance in speeding up road clearance.

----

9. SOME JOTTINGS BY AN INFANTRY BATTALION COMMANDER

Since my return from North Africa, I have been asked by several people for impressions from the point of view of an infantry battalion commander.

I make no claim to original ideas, and shall be merely quoting from practical experience, and I have no doubt that a large number of other battalion commanders have employed similar methods and will agree with the majority of my comments.

My first comment is that although modern war has produced no change in the principles of war, the tempo calls for much quicker reactions, which must be borne in mind throughout all training. The system of training laid down for the infantry, if carried out with understanding, could not be better.

Briefly listed below are some of the chief points which seem to me to call for particular attention during training :—

1. Leadership—The number of casualties that occur during battle on any scale calls for large reserves of leaders and we must, therefore, aim at producing the maximum number of leaders during the training period. I made it my job to try and make every man capable of acting as a leader in emergency. One occasionally makes a bad error of judgment in selecting leaders during training, and these errors must be ruthlessly corrected as soon as noted.

2. Toughness and physical fitness.

3. The ability to march long distances as quickly as possible, and then dig-in and use one's weapons quickly.

4. The ability to exist on odd meals at odd hours, and to take no heed of the weather.

5. The necessity for care of arms.

6. The organization of rest periods.

And finally and in my opinion one of the most important
7. The creation of the very highest esprit de corps.
After these few general headings, the rest of my impressions can best be dealt with as follows :—
The Training Period.
Action—Before, During and After actual Battle.

Training Period.

The Object.—To produce a team capable of carrying out their leaders' wishes quickly without fluster, and to apply various drills to the ground over which they must work, with the ultimate task of destroying the enemy completely.

The first thing in my opinion is to ensure that no one exists in the battalion, who is not thoroughly acquainted with this object and who does not fully realise that it is his duty to help in achieving the object. Every item that is taught, either from the manuals or from the various army schools, has a very definite bearing on the production of a first-class battalion.

Secondly, what is most necessary is that all leaders, and potential leaders, are continuously given instruction and are tested as often as possible both in leadership and in passing on what they have learnt to their men.

Thirdly, everybody should be capable of feats of great physical endurance. In our division everybody had to march 10 miles in two hours and 6 miles in one hour. In my battalion I insisted that not only should they be able to do this, but also be able to engage the enemy and destroy him with their weapons at the end of it. Apart from anything else, the fact that the men knew that they could do this, gave them all a great feeling of confidence and superiority. In our own case we were fortunate in being stationed during training just six miles distant from a rifle range, but even if a range is not available, some improvisation should be made in order to test the men's ability to shoot at the end of their march.

At this point, I would like to say that when we first started on this toughening-up process, I was not at all sure that we were not perhaps rather overdoing it, but when I had satisfied myself that it was very much in our interests always to be able to do just a little more than the people next to us could do, I drove my own battalion, as I have already stated, to doing that little bit more. I know that a number of people serving under me thought that I was perhaps rather overdoing it. Well the proof of the pudding is in the eating, and I hate being thanked by many people since we have been in contact with the enemy for having given them just that extra bit of confidence that this toughening process does produce.

During training, particularly at the end, every man should always move with, and become accustomed to handling, all the equipment, ammunition, and weapons, etc., that he will be expected to carry on the battlefield. It is better if anything to overdo this rather than underdo it, and I was particularly glad that I had practised my battalion not only in this way, but also in marching with a pack, and full load, for when we landed in Africa we were faced with a 15-mile march fully loaded, with greatcoats, blankets, waterproof sheets, packs, etc., from the quayside to our rest area. The men had been at sea for a considerable period, and they would certainly have been completely defeated if they had not known they could do it.

During training it is also very necessary to stress periodically the hygiene side of war. Casualties on the battlefield are very hard to replace, and it is bad enough to lose men by enemy action, without losing them also by unnecessary ailments, and it is, therefore, every man's duty to take every possible precaution to keep himself fit. To help in this we had several lectures by medical officers, and army films were also shown, but however much is done, it is the junior leader who finally makes or mars this side of the picture, and it cannot be overstressed. Included in this side of training should be the necessity for water discipline. Some theatres of war demand this more than others, but everyone should be well aware of the necessity for good water discipline, and how everyone can help.

I am not attempting to go into detail about all types of infantry training, but I am merely emphasising a few particular items which should certainly not be overlooked at any time.

Listed below are a few points that require attention before, during, and after battle, and if these are considered during training, they will then become automatic during the fighting.

Before Battle.

Deception.—Under this heading, should come d e c e i v i n g the enemy by every possible means, as to (a) your whereabouts and (b) your intentions. Every man must realise that he plays a very big part in this, for careless movement, failure to disguise himself or his position, the lighting of fires and smoking, bad track discipline, failure to hide his weapons, vehicles, etc., all let the team down. After a very short time, this is well realised, and immediate camouflage becomes almost automatic, but in the early days the novice is likely to pay with his life, and that of his comrades, if he does not think about it. The deception of the enemy with regard to your future plans, and anything you can do to bluff him, must also receive very careful attention. In our battalion, we made the intelligence officer act as the commanding officer of the force directly opposed to the battalion, and each morning he was asked to give his point of view of the German side of the picture. We then considered it and used such counter-measures as we thought most suitable. I only quote this as an example because I do feel that someone must be constantly thinking from the enemy point of view, in order that we can always be prepared for eventualities.

Anticipation.—Always think ahead, and be prepared for the unexpected. We noticed on several occasions that orders were issued for moves in most unexpected directions, at very short notice. For instance on one occasion the whole of the battalion transport system had to be converted to mule transport, and if this eventuality had not been foreseen and mule loading tables had not been prepared, great confusion might have ensued. As far as possible higher formations kept one informed and warned of forthcoming events, but many times one had to ferret for information, and I always encourage company commanders to seek out such information from battalion, and I definitely worried brigade whenever I felt we were not being given enough information.

Testing of Weapons.—EVERY DAY weapons should be tested, particularly during any extremes of weather, and the greatest attention paid to care of arms. In the Great War 1914-1918 every man was taught that the rifle was his best friend, and in this war everyone must also be made to realise that his weapon is a very real comrade, when it comes to the point, but like all good friends they repay kindly attention. When testing weapons give the men some definite object to aim at ; never let them waste ammunition. In our brigade we had a motto "Every Round a Funeral", and these daily tests were the most excellent opportunity to improve one's marksmanship.

Study of Enemy Positions.—I do not feel it is necessary for me to stress the importance of studying enemy positions, lines of approach, ground, etc., but it is not a bad thing during the training period to call for written reports from all one's leaders periodically on such matters. This should also be done at first and last light, and everyone should become accustomed to knowing how light and darkness affect their vision and appreciation of ground. Use of field glasses in the dark is perhaps worth mentioning, and also the value of the compass.

Digging-in.—I have already mentioned the necessity for digging-in, and it will not take anyone long before this becomes a matter of routine, but I would stress the necessity for quick digging of slit trenches, because should the enemy locate you, it will not be many moments before his mortars make their presence felt, and whilst on this subject, I would mention the fact that the Boche are very quick at moving their mortars or machine guns from one position to another. It is when you think you have located them that you find they are no longer there, and the converse should apply, and we should always have alternative positions already prepared.

Co-operation.—The co-operation of all arms is a principle that none of us should lose sight of, and yet it does require constantly rubbing in to all leaders, that they should never prepare for battle, without considering how they may make best use of all the different weapons at their disposal, and close liaison between those who handle the various weapons is most desirable. I can think of one particular occasion in which the battery supporting our battalion knew most of our men, and the officers actually lived in my headquarters. Thus to all intents and purposes we spoke the same language, and when the battle was joined, one could not have wished for a closer co-operation and understanding than we had from our gunners.

Keep Everyone in the Picture.—I would again stress the necessity for every man in the battalion and all supporting formations, knowing the plan and what is expected of them. This must reach every man and not be just a matter for the leaders. During battle, leaders are killed and if the men do not know what is expected of them, the commander cannot expect them to carry out his orders.

Administration.—This requires very careful thought and the feeding of the men before, during and after the battle produces many problems. Providing one is able to, it is not a bad thing to have one officer detailed to give this his constant attention and to work out ways and means, and so relieve those responsible for the planning and actual fighting, though naturally they should always keep in the picture, and must know full details.

During Battle.

Control.—Keep everyone on the right leg as long as possible, and insure that everybody knows what is happening on their flanks, etc.

Do not put all your eggs in one basket. In the First Army, there was a very definite list of people who did not go into battle for example, seconds-in-command of the battalions and companies were kept back together with certain selected NCOs and specialists. This was highly desirable, as these people replaced casualties either during the battle or immediately afterwards.

Dispersal.—The need for dispersal of headquarters must also be remembered. On the day I was wounded, I had fortunately remembered this rule, and had divided even my advance headquarters into two parts, and although my adjutant who was accompanying me was within a 100 yards of me, he was not actually at my elbow, when the mortar shell burst. The same thing applies to the company headquarters which should never be all bunched together.

Drill and Maintenance of Momentum.—The correct application of battle drill requires no stressing, but any failure on the part of the men to observe the elementary rules of maintaining their distance, all-round protection, and the avoidance of obvious machine-gun targets, will meet with disaster. However, no amount of drills will provide one to suit every occasion, and it is as well that the men should realise during their training that all drills practised are more in the nature of suggestions than hard and fast rules. During the battle one will quickly appreciate the value of having trained as many leaders as possible and the maintenance of momentum by the individual is worth a tremendous amount. Here again the fact that every man knows what is expected of him, and the fact that he has been trained to lead if necessary, should prevent any individual stickiness that sometimes occurs. No one must be allowed to stop because of casualties ; the stretcher-bearers will deal with these, and it must be understood by all ranks that until the battle is won, every man's job is to drive on to the objective. The lesser wounded will tend those who are unable to look after themselves. The stretcher bearers will come up and remove those men, but on no account should a fit man fall out of the move forward, until he is satisfied that the objective is captured and only then if ordered to do so, or with permission from an officer. It stands to reason that if anybody hesitates or stops when casualties occur, the enemy will take full advantage of it, and the plight of the casualties in such a case would be very bad indeed. The necessity for all-round protection has been so constantly rubbed in to us all, that I feel it hardly necessary to mention it, nevertheless it might be just as well to say that flanks and rear have been forgotten on occasions, and also protection against aircraft, but a battalion that has been well trained will not overlook these points.

Information.—The passing of information back to headquarters is so vitally important, that one hopes it has been sufficiently emphasised in the past, but it is very difficult to make many people realize that even when they are pushing on and everything is going well, and that there are no enemy in certain places, that this is just the very time that headquarters is longing to know of these facts, and it must be a rule to keep headquarters constantly informed throughout all phases of the battle.

At this point I would like to say how very impressed I was at all times with the splendid work of our signal platoon, who under the most difficult conditions kept our communications going when it seemed as though they could not possibly do so, and the signal platoon in a battalion is so important, that no amount of trouble taken in their training can be too much.

Miscellaneous.—Should it become necessary at any time to withdraw, it must be a point of honour that no equipment of any sort is left behind. This was clearly understood, and should never happen in a good battalion. Before discussing the points after battle, it may interest everyone to know how very valuable the use of the bayonet has been in more than one attack in which we took part, so this weapon should receive just as much attention during the training period as others.

On all occasions, headquarters (battalion and company) must have duty rosters prepared, and junior officers must be trained to make decisions on minor matters, if necessary during the rest period of their commanders.

After Battle.

Reorganization.—The reorganization and regrouping of the battalion immediately after battle and the preparation for counter-attack has been constantly brought to our notice by everyone.

Reverse Slopes.—The Boche invariably had their own position and possibly also a position on a forward slope already registered, so that within half-an-hour of their leaving these positions they could bring down fire on them. These positions should therefore always be avoided, and positions dug in on the reverse slope, as quickly as possible.

Feeding and Vigilance.—Once a position has been reorganised, food is usually one of the first thoughts, but on no account should vigilance be allowed to get slack. During this period, all meals must be staggered, and the very keenest observation of any enemy likely to approach must be kept up.

Casualties and Reinforcements.—All casualties must be got away, and such reinforcements as are available pulled in as quickly as possible, but all this is well-known and everyday routine.

Conclusion.—The foregoing is very briefly the main impressions and lessons that I learnt as a battalion commander during my few months in North Africa. Of course, there are many other lessons and I have no doubt that many of the lessons that I have mentioned are well known to most people, but on the off-chance that they may be of some use in helping a few men to avoid mistakes, I feel that it is worth while passing them on.

10. BATTLE INSTRUCTIONS

This section contains extracts from the operational instructions issued by a division as a result of experience in battle in NORTH AFRICA. It has been included because it brings out forcibly that there is little difference—between Jungle Warfare and Warfare in other parts of the world.

Discipline.—Recent operations have proved once again that good unit discipline is the foundation of success. No degree of skill or enthusiasm can make up for lack of it. Commanding officers will ensure that at all times only the highest standard of discipline is accepted. This will always be reflected in the bearing of units, their saluting and turn-out and the cleanliness and efficiency of their arms and equipment. Officers must especially take care that NCOs tolerate no laxity of discipline.

Holding Position in Contact with the Enemy.

All-round Defence.—This must be literally accepted and acted upon as long as there are two men left, who must, if necessary, fight back-to-back.

Company positions must invariably be sited for all-round defence, and an approach by the enemy from what is in daily use regarded as the back must NOT be allowed to alarm or discourage a garrison. It must be got down to every man that infiltration will not only occur—but should be encouraged.

An enemy who has got round behind cannot get away from a determined defence.

During training men must be made familiar with this feeling of being surrounded. The alarm felt on occasions at a comparatively weak infiltration probably arises from neglect of this factor in training. Umpires are apt to wipe out at once a sub-unit surrounded.

It will often be advantageous to refrain from occupying a somewhat obvious tactical feature if it can be dominated by fire from the flanks. It should be used to tempt the enemy on to a position where he can be destroyed.

Holding of Fire.—This demands a high standard of fire discipline but it must be insisted upon by all arms.

There have been several British patrols—both by day and night—that disappeared completely. It was nearly always because the enemy held his fire until the patrol was right into his position. Few German patrols have been so treated.

When men are allotted fire positions, clear orders will be given about the opening of fire. The exact line where the enemy will first be engaged by fire will be marked on the ground either by natural objects such as the edge of a field or by a red board 6 inches square hidden from the enemy's side. This line should be near enough to our fire positions to ensure that a considerable body of the enemy is exposed in the open before fire is opened. Separate orders will be issued about opening fire on patrols, which should be allowed to approach near enough to make sure the whole patrol is destroyed.

Once fire becomes general in repelling an attack snipers should concentrate on picking off enemy leaders, machine gunners, and observation posts well back in the enemy's advance.

Our artillery also is prone to shoot at the least sign of movement.

If the enemy does move by day, all arms must hold their fire and keep him under observation to see what he is up to. If, for example, he is trying to lay on a working party—let it get started to work. Valuable information may be gleaned from an examination of his activities. Once the party has got down to work, it can efficaciously be engaged by a concentration of artillery.

Anti-tank gunners have in recent operations shown the highest standard of fire discipline and held their fire until a killing range was reached.

"Hold your fire" must be ingrained into all ranks of all arms.

Movement and Alertness by Day and Night.—The amount of movement seen in German positions by day was remarkably small.

Infantry in particular must be severely disciplined and trained into remaining motionless by day in front line positions. Once troops have suffered under mortar fire they learn this lesson ; but it is an expensive and useless sacrifice of life for every fresh draft to have to learn it by experience. Commanding officers must impress upon their sub-units that this lesson must be a rigid drill.

A few observation posts, well concealed, with covered approaches and communications (either by voice or No. 18 set) are all that need be manned by day.

If an enemy patrol is reported, cunning must be employed ; only the necessary light automatics, mortars or sections should be "stood to." To "stand to" the whole battalion will almost certainly warn the enemy.

Conversely, by night, alertness must be at its highest pitch, and at night very few can expect to sleep in front line positions.

Unit commanders will pay special attention to ensuring that all junior commanders and leaders do in fact get their rest by day. Essential daily routine such as rifle inspection, checking of returns, etc., should as far as possible be done during "stand to".

One officer only per company should usually be on duty by day—and unit and formation commanders must deal with him. Otherwise company and platoon commanders are up all night and get no rest by day.

Selection and Organisation of Positions.—Once an objective is captured it is extremely important to organise it and dig in : it will probably be subjected to heavy mortar and machine gun fire early, and a counter-attack will follow.

To speed up this reorganisation and occupation, the following steps will be taken :—

    (a) The objective must be carefully studied beforehand, either from an observation post, from an air photo, or on the map. The general framework of the projected positions should be known to commanders of leading companies and platoons.

    (b) When the objective is reached, a quick look to confirm or modify the planned occupation is all that can be done.

    (c) Usually most of the positions to be dug should be on a reverse slope, as this will often prevent enemy mortar fire being observed and accurate. An exception to this rule will be when strong enemy positions are captured. These will usually be on their reverse slope—which on capture becomes a forward slope. Even though these are on a forward slope, it is probably better to occupy them if they are still good enough to give shelter from mortar fire. But even then, positions on the reverse slope should be dug by reserve platoons and companies, so that forward troops can be thinned out into them.

A clear decision must be given on where the position is to be held by night; i. e., on a forward or reverse slope. Usually the best results will be obtained by reinforcing at night, with automatics and grenade throwers, the observation posts held by day. The remainder of the company or platoons should be ready to go forward in immediate counter-attack and advance to meet the enemy as he gets near these posts.

The same tactics will often be decisive by day.

(d) If a reverse slope is selected for the main position, it is most important that strong observation posts be dug or blasted with a good view forward and to the flanks. In extreme cases it may be necessary to cover the digging of these with smoke. This can often provide useful registration for artillery or mortars.

(e) Weapons must be sited at once. Time cannot be afforded for long reconnaissance for ideal positions. They must, however, provide all round defence.

(f) Patrols should be sent out in front and to the flanks.

(g) It must be remembered that keen eyes will be watching all visible dispositions. It will rarely be possible in the short time that can be spared to site all anti-tank guns and machine guns unspotted. Arrangements must therefore be made for further reconnaissance, and fresh positions should be dug in the first hours of darkness after capture, so that anti-tank guns and machine guns can be moved.

(h) It cannot be over-emphasised that, with proper support, it is comparatively easy to take any given position. The difficulty always is to hold it. Therefore the more thoroughly arrangements are thought out beforehand for occupation, and the more these arrangements can be reduced to a drill, the better advantage will be taken of the period of confusion when the enemy is not sure whether his own troops are still there or not. Provided that observation patrols are pushed just clear of it, smoke can often be usefully employed to prolong this uncertainty. On at least one occasion smoke, put down by us on a position to cover our withdrawal, finally decided the enemy to abandon a position for which he had fought tenaciously.

11. SIGNALS IN BATTLE

Siting of HQ.

The lesson that signals must always be consulted by the staff before sites for headquarters and main axes of advance are selected, is one upon which stress is constantly being laid. In recent operations there have been instances which indicate that this lesson has not yet been thoroughly learnt, with resultant failure in selection of the best sites from the point of view of communications ; on these occasions signals personnel had sometimes to be diverted hurriedly from other urgent work elsewhere.

In order to make line communications efficient, it is essential that headquarters should be sited, before a battle, well forward in relation to subordinate headquarters. Signals units from army downwards have neither the personnel nor equipment to provide long distance telephone circuits. Moreover, such forward siting will probably obviate the need for the headquarters to move forward during the battle.

Tactical headquarters, when formed, must be regarded as potential sites for main headquarters, and should, therefore, be established close to a subordinate headquarters. Thus the tactical headquarters can be quickly connected with an existing line system, which can also be utilised for the main headquarters when the latter moves forward.

Co-operation Between Signals and Staff.

Effective command can only be exercised through good communications. Staffs and signals are therefore essentially partners in the technique of staff work. Unless the two elements work in harmony as part of a single team, full efficiency from communications will never be obtained.

A formation's signal office must be regarded as the nerve centre of the formation's organisation for command. Successful handling of the signal office is dependent on the combined efforts of both signals and staff ; without mutual co-operation the efforts of the best trained signal units will be in vain. Difficulties often arise when lower formations and units are switched in battle to the command of another formation. On these occasions the combination of signals and staffs is broken up, and there is a corresponding loss in efficiency.

Concentration of the Signals Effort.

The principle of concentration of effort applies just as much to signals as it does to other arms. There is, however, a tendency for all arms to regard themselves as entitled to a certain scale of communications— to so many wireless sets and frequencies, or to line communications laid out to a standard pattern.

The signals effort must be concentrated upon the main tasks. For instance, communications with a body of troops allocated to an important feature may have to be doubled or trebled at the expense of communications elsewhere. In extreme circumstances it may be necessary to allot as many as three No. 18 wireless sets to a single infantry company, or two FOOs each with his own communications.

It follows, therefore, that, in order to avoid duplication of effort and to ensure that the available resources are applied economically, the signals plan should be co-ordinated on as high a level as practicable, and that the whole signal resources of a formation must be used in the way best calculated to further the commander's plan.

Relative Merits of Wireless and Line.

There is still not sufficient appreciation of the relative merits of wireless and line, and of how to adjust the balance between them.

Wireless has the advantages of speed, mobility, flexibility, ability to overcome physical distances, and power to broadcast. The use of wireless enables a commander to retain control in a mobile battle ; it also enables the services to dispose in the forward areas, and keep in touch with administrative elements, such as medical and recovery detachments, which otherwise would have to remain tied to those areas where line communications exist. On the other hand, wireless is not secure, is liable to interference, can handle only a limited amount of traffic, and is sensitive to ground and atmospheric interference. While, therefore, the possibilities of wireless must be exploited to the full, and formations must be prepared to work entirely on wireless when necessary, wireless by itself cannot provide the comprehensive and secure system of communications required during deliberate operations or static periods, nor handle the volume of traffic that has to be transmitted in rear areas. Moreover, there will be periods, when, in order to avoid jeopardising surprise, wireless silence must be imposed.

From the staff point of view the telephone provides the best form of communication and, in rear areas, or for the initial stages of any large scale attack when large quantities of artillery are under centralised control, line communications are essential. Considerable time is needed, however, to lay a comprehensive line system, while its maintenance in the forward area during battle is difficult. Telephone routes are liable to be cut by shell fire or bombing, while whole sections may be carried away by tracked or wheeled vehicles. Important links should, therefore, be duplicated, and in the battle area should always be supplemented by wireless.

Wireless.

The importance of some of the old lessons regarding the use of wireless is still not appreciated :

(a) Effective control by wireless in battle depends on good wireless discipline. It is not sufficient that officers and signal operators should have been taught how to use the wireless ; they must also receive constant practice. Officers at all levels still require more practice in the use of RT. This practice must be continuous, and must go on during quiet spells in the field no less than in training at home.

(b) Officers require more practice in key conversation. Few officers seem to realise that, although atmospheric conditions may make RT impossible, wireless communication may often still be possible by WT.

(c) The need for careful allotment of frequencies, and of strict frequency discipline, becomes very apparent when formations converge from a broad on to a narrow front.

(d) A higher standard of training of regimental signallers is required in the use of the No. 18 set. The results obtained by infantry units have been very uneven. In some units the sets worked uniformly well, in other units the results were quite inexcusably poor.

Message Priorities.

The abuse of priorities merely defeats its own object which is to upgrade the speed of transmission. Staff officers must not assume that, because the contents of a message are operationally important, that message automatically needs priority in transmission. A message containing highly important operational matter will need no priority at all, if it is unnecessary for recipients to get it urgently, while, conversely, a priority will sometimes be required for a message containing routine matter.

SPECIAL FEATURES

12. THE PRINCIPLES OF INSTRUCTION

What the Instructor has to do.

This article is intended as a guide for instructors. A very large part of army life is spent in training, and all officers, warrant officers and N. C. Os. have to spend a great deal of their time in instruction. It is therefore important that they should study the art, and should try and make themselves good instructors.

We all know that training parades in the Army are often dull and boring. There is no reason why they should be so, provided that the instructor has taken trouble to study how to liven them up and make them interesting. It can be done, and it is your job to do it.

In military training we are aiming at making each individual fit to take his appointed place on the battlefield. The conditions of modern war make such demands on the individual that each man must be able to think and act for himself. This means that every man must be as mentally fit as he is physically fit, with all his qualities developed to the highest possible standard. We have taken a lot of trouble to make our Army physically fit. It needs just as much care and trouble to make it mentally fit. That should be our first aim in training.

Development of the Individual.

At the beginning of this war we used to rely on making our men physically fit mainly through physical training, route marching and games. Training in general was built on conditions which required more "mass discipline" than individual effort, although the need for the latter had begun to make itself felt. Our methods of instruction were therefore rather stereotyped, and were not really suited to bringing out individual mental activity.

No two minds are the same, and each mind requires a slightly different form of "exercise" to produce the best results. A good instructor will always be studying the development of the individual minds of his class, and will be thinking out ways of getting the highest degree of mental alertness.

To do this he must work hard to make his class interested in what they are doing. No one will learn if he is not interested, or does not know how this particular piece of training is to help him the better to be an efficient soldier. **On the other hand if a man leaves a lesson feeling that he has taken a personal part in it, and has possibly contributed something himself, he will probably not only remember what he has learnt, but will look forward with keenness to the next lesson.**

Making the Mind Work.

If a man's mind is to be kept actively at work it must be continually given problems with which it is capable of dealing. A man by using his ordinary commonsense can build up his own knowledge provided he starts from something which he knows already.

A good instructor will therefore start by finding out what knowledge a man has already got about the subject under discussion. He can find this out by putting simple questions to him, or possibly he may have already been teaching the man his previous knowledge, and can put him in the right frame of mind by questioning him about the last lesson. This method will also have the advantage of showing the man that his training is continuous.

Having found the basis on which to start, the instructor can then, by question or suggestion, guide the man towards working out for himself the next step in the knowledge he is to acquire. **To do this well the instructor must have prepared his lesson thoroughly.** He should know something about the characteristics of the man whom he is instructing, and he should frame his teaching so as to make the best use of these characteristics. In other words he must apply his methods to suit the type of man with whom he has to deal. This requires thought and patience. But it will in the end produce the best results, because the man will be thinking for himself.

Man is a naturally curious animal. Excite his curiosity and his mind at once begins to "tick over". This is what you must aim at doing in training.

Explaining Why Things Happen.

One of the errors which is often made in army training is that we are too much inclined to tell a man what a thing is, rather than what it does. We teach a man to name the parts of a Bren gun, rather than to explain why each part is the shape it is. **That little word "why?" should appear very frequently in all forms of instruction.** Reasons are so much more important than facts, and a man who has worked out the reasons for any particular thing has begun to get a real " working knowledge " of the subject.

It is surprising what even an apparently stupid man can work out for himself if his curiosity is aroused. So the instructor should find something which is already within his pupil's knowledge and by testing and probing into the man's way of thinking get him to puzzle out what happens next.

This is an important principle in training and it can be applied in some measure to every subject which has to be taught as part of military instruction. To be successful, the instructor must start by assuming that the men have minds of their own, and that it is possible for them to get those minds actively to work if their interest can be aroused.

The Maintenance of Interest.

The ordinary man is so built that his mind is most active when he is up against something or somebody. The feeling that he has got to pit his own mind against some form of competition automatically stirs him on to a greater effort. This is a thing to remember whenever you are thinking out how you are going to plan your instruction.

If an instructor stands up before a squad and repeats the lessons word for word as he has learnt them from his manual it has an unfailing effect on the men. While you are

teaching watch your men's eyes. It is the surest way of telling whether you are getting your stuff across or not.

If you have only got one man to teach it is fairly easy to keep his mind alert. The more men you have the more difficult it is to find ways of keeping them constantly alert mentally.

The most important thing is to make each man feel that he is personally concerned in the subject of instruction. You can do this by continually asking the different members of the squad in turn questions, from the answers to which you can build up the information you want. Your questions should not be regular, but they should always be addressed to a man by name, and not to the class as a whole. Ask the question first and name the man afterwards in order to keep the class alert.

Do not pin on one man all the time, either because you think you will get the answer quicker or because you think he is inattentive. Remember that if a man is inattentive it is very largely your fault. Make your questions crisp and direct, but keep your tone friendly.

Let Them Teach Each Other.

If your subject matter makes it difficult to keep all the men attentive yourself, then you should work them in twos or threes and make them keep each other's minds alert. Mutual criticism and even mutual teaching can be started at a very early stage in training. As soon as they have got some elementary knowledge the attempt to teach each other will tend at once to an improvement in their own knowledge. Moreover, the slight spirit of competition which enters into it keeps up interest in itself. This can be applied to the dullest subjects with success.

We are often troubled with shortage of training equipment which means that only a few men in a squad can really be instructed at one time. Turn the other on to some other work for the time being, give them a task to work out, or encourage them to teach each other. NEVER allow them to stand or sit by as passive spectators. Your whole effort must be directed towards making the man realise that he can find out a great deal for himself if he only tries.

Whenever possible men should be given a chance of really handling for themselves the equipment in which they are being instructed. Above all it is far more important that they should know the reason for things than the actual things. Those useful words "Why?" and "How?" should roll frequently off your tongue. It is the answers to those questions which really make a man think.

The Eye to See.

Most of us have a very poor command of language. We can express ourselves in terms which we understand, but it is not always so easy to be sure that the listeners are interpreting what we say in the way that we mean. But if we can show somebody what we are talking about, what we mean, or what we are trying to do, there is a very much smaller chance of misunderstanding.

The instructor should therefore try, whenever possible, to illustrate this teaching by practical methods. These may vary from merely showing the men a weapon or some inanimate object about which they are being taught, to a full dress demonstration in the form of a little play or sketch All these are most useful forms of instruction because they appeal to the eye, which records much more accurately and permanently than the ear.

But in using these "visual aids" to instruction, the instructor must be careful to get the best effect from them. If, for instance, you are showing a Sten gun to a class for the first time do not be content with just letting them have a look at it. Encourage them to handle it, to turn it about and examine it carefully, and even to try and find out for themselves how it works. If you are showing a working model of anything be sure and show exactly how it works. In a demonstration lay emphasis on the particular things you want to teach, but do not neglect the background.

It is sometimes useful to demonstrate the wrong way as well as the right way of doing things. There is a pitfall here which should be avoided. Many instructors in their anxiety to put on a good "turn" give

a hopelessly exaggerated display of things going wrong. Incidents are staged which could not possibly happen in a well conducted unit, and everybody has a good laugh. But at the same time everybody is subconsciously recording the fact that the things shown are completely unreal, and therefore they do not learn from them. There is no harm in a good laugh, in fact many parades would be the better for one. But there is quite sufficient which goes wrong in everyday life to demonstrate and to raise a laugh without turning to the ridiculous or impossible.

Learning by Practical Experience.

All "visual aids" should be as simple as possible. Complicated models or diagrams or a long demonstration which smothers the real purpose, are apt to confuse the minds of the men under instruction. Models and diagrams which the instructor or the men can make for themselves will usually arouse more interest than those provided from other sources, because the man has a feeling that he is more personally concerned in them. An instructor can, with a little thought, improvise most ingenious illustrations of what he is trying to teach from the most ordinary and commonplace materials.

Instructional films play an important part in training, but again the best use of them requires careful study. Most films will be of greater value if they can be helped out by practical work. Thus it will often be a good thing to show a film and then take the men outside to discuss it and to carry out in practice what it is trying to teach. Then take them back for another look at the film to check up on what they have been doing and to correct mistakes. Again it is an error to look upon films as a useful bit of training to put on suddenly on a wet day. They should take their place in a progressive scheme of training and should be marked down for showing in their proper place.

All "visual aids" to training require thought and planning if they are going to be a success.—If they are used in a hurry or haphazard they will not produce the real value which they should do.

Planning and Preparation.

Without careful planning and preparation no instructor can give of his best and very few can do anything useful at all. A lesson built up in a haphazard careless way is worse than useless. It is probably harmful.

If you do not prepare your lesson you cannot expect to be able to meet effectively the difficulties which you will always find in taking any

.class. Therefore it is worth while trying to make your preparation on lines which should be fairly well known to anyone who has to tackle military problems. After you have tried it seriously for a little while you will find your preparation and planning coming quite naturally to you.

You cannot afford not to have some careful thought out plan before you face your squad. If you have not taken any trouble they will soon find you out, and they will at once lose interest.

Do not make the mistake of thinking that, because you have given a lesson once, it will not need planning and preparation the next time. It may not need quite so much, but the conditions will be different each time you give it, and these differences will need to be studied if you are to give of your best.

Remember that there are three things vital to any instructor before he starts on a lesson : a real knowledge of his subject, careful preparation of the lesson, and a studied plan of present-ation. These alone can give the instructor a well-founded con-fidence in himself.

Sequence of Instruction.

Whatever plan you may make for a particular lesson it is always wise to follow a definite system on which to base it. Experience has shown that there is a definite order of doing things which helps to present a lesson in a clear and logical way and therefore to attract and maintain the man's interest.

It has already been shown that the best results can be obtained by building up on the man's existing knowledge, and getting him, if possible, to develop the lesson himself by the working of his own mind. If he is to do this he must know first what the lesson is designed to do. Therefore the instructor should start by saying what the lesson is about and why the man will be better by knowing it. Having done this he must then link it up with something within his pupil's knowledge. If the lesson is one of a series, the instructor should recall the subject matter of the previous lesson or lessons by well chosen questions to his class. If he is starting a new subject, he should try and find some point of knowledge in the minds of the class from which he can start building. Very often this can be done by reference to some ordinary thing of everyday life, from which a comparison can be made with the subject he wishes to teach. Care must be taken, however, that these compari-sons are not too far-fetched.

It is usually as well at this point to explain to the class, or to get from them, the "war purpose" of the lesson. The statement of the "war purpose" of the lesson may also help the instructor to make sure that he has got his "planning" right.

Very often a demonstration of what you are trying to teach will put your class early into the picture. The time for such a demonstration is at the beginning of the lesson after the preliminary work described above. **The demonstration should be clear, short and snappy.** It is unwise at this stage to demonstrate the wrong way of doing things. You are trying to put correct ideas into the men's head. Do not muddle him up with incorrect methods. The time for demonstrations of the "wrong" way comes when the pupil has sufficient knowledge to be able to distinguish for himself between "right" and "wrong". Do not waste time over detail. Just show how the thing should be done and leave detail to the next stage.

Mastering the Subject.

The next stage is the actual period of study. It may be by discussion, by reasoning, by practice, or by investigation of the subject shown in the demonstration. It is during this period in particular that the instructor should do everything in his power to keep the minds of his whole class active and alert. They should be placed, whether on parade in a squad or grouped for study, sufficiently far from him to be able to watch them all, and near enough for them to take a personal part in the lesson, and, if necessary, to handle the subject of study for themselves and to see the smallest details. Make sure that they are as comfortable as circumstances allow you to make them. Discomfort distracts attention, and this is what you are trying to avoid.

Having reached the required stage in instruction you must always be careful to drive home the lessons which should have been learnt. This is done by repeating or summarizing the main features of the lesson as briefly and clearly as possible. Try and think out a way of putting them so that they will imprint themselves on the minds of your class. Here again simplicity will serve you far better than any tricky catch-words or phrases. Wind up your period by again pointing out the continuity from what has already been learnt, and by emphasizing once more the war purpose of the lesson.

Make up your mind in your "planning" how much time you are going to allow for each phase. But do not allow yourself to be hurried into skimping some important part of your subject because your time table is going wrong. It is better to finish short of your objective than to arrive there without having "mopped up" thoroughly on the way.

Experience will soon put you into the way of organising and controlling your lesson. **But the time factor must be an essential part of your plan.**

Lecturing.

Every instructor must be prepared to give lectures on subjects which can only be dealt with by that means. Even in lecture subjects it is possible to draw the class into taking some part in the instruction by means of questions and discussion, and opportunities for doing this should be watched for and taken. But there are certain points of which an instructor should take note when he is faced with a straightforward lecture.

Planning and preparation are just as important for lectures as for other forms of instruction. Clear thought as to the object of the lecture will save a great deal of time and will help you to lay the subject matter out on an organised plan. Above all things at this stage you should watch the time factor. Very few subjects are so absorbing or lectures so good that they can occupy the attention of a class for more than 30 to 40 minutes. Moreover you should leave plenty of time at the end for questions and discussion, which you may have to provoke yourself.

Every lecturer will be wise to prepare notes of some sort for his subject. Whether these notes are short reminders or a rather longer precis must depend on the taste and ability of the individual. NEVER write out your lecture as you intend to give it, and then read it to your class. There are not many of us who can talk very well, but the number of those who can read well is even smaller.

Plan your notes out under headings and make up your mind how long you are going to spend on each. Then keep your eye on a clock or watch while you are talking and make sure you keep within your allotted time. If you find you are being quicker than you expected do not try and spin it out. It is far better to finish early than to start "padding". That leads to boredom. Incidentally tell your class if you want them to take notes or not.

Face your class and talk to them. If you see any of them becoming inattentive try and direct your talk to them, or maintain silence until the inattentive sense something is wrong. Watch your class as a whole and try and tune yourself into their "wave lengths". **If you see attention wandering remember that it is probably your fault. You must compel them to listen to you by your own arts.**

How to Acquire Confidence.

Study your voice and attitude, and study those of other people, particularly of lecturers whom you find interesting. Try and see how they get their effects. **Above all avoid "mannerisms" or nervous actions** which do more than almost anything else to distract the attention of the class. Strolling about, fiddling with chalk or pencils or other apparatus, clutching a reading desk or chair and swaying about with it are all common habits, and they are all fatal to good lecturing.

Keep still, unless you have a definite purpose for moving.
Use gestures if they come natural to you, but don't become too acrobatic. If you are inexperienced in lecturing it is very good practice to give your lecture out loud to yourself in front of a looking glass, and to study your "effects". This also helps you to judge your timing. But you had better not do it where your friends can see you.

Your class must be able both to see and hear. If you have blackboards, diagrams, models, or other apparatus, prepare them beforehand and make sure that the lighting is such that they can be seen from all parts of your class room. You may often want to hide up your apparatus so as not to distract the class before the time for showing it arrives. In that case plan the "unveiling" so that it can be done with the least interruption. **Provide yourself with a pointer beforehand, and put it where you can find it.**

If you have to draw, stop lecturing while you are doing it.
Your actions will muffle your voice and distract the class. If you are

no artist have a thin outline drawing prepared and draw in as required. If you have to point something out on a map or diagram pause in your talking while you do so. Be sure you know where the thing is to which you wish to point. You must often have seen a lecturer trying to top to a blackboard with his back to the audience, or gazing blankly at a map while he tries to find the place, and you know how bad the effect is.

Speak clearly and fairly slowly. Try to pronounce each syllable of the words you are using. And do not shout or use your "barrack square" way of talking when you are lecturing. It is usually as well to ask after a few minutes if you can be heard. Remember that it always takes an audience a minute or two to "tune in" to a speaker's voice so pay particular attention to your opening sentences. Be careful not to "drone", but try and introduce some expression in your voice.

If you don't feel you have been successful at first do not be discouraged. Go on studying and trying and you will get better at it.

"Know Thyself".

Over the doorway of one of the famous colleges of philosophy in ancient Greece were carved two words : "Know Thyself". This motto is a very good one for instructors, because it is the man who has studied himself carefully who will know how to fit his subject to his individual style. A good instructor always has something of the play-actor in him, and it is according to how he plays his part whether he makes or mars his effects.

Here are some simple rules for an instructor to observe. They have been built up by study of the most common faults in instruction at one of the large army training centres.

1. NEVER TRY AND INSTRUCT WITHOUT FIRST PRE-PARING YOUR WORK. You may want an hour — you may want two minutes, but you will want some time. Even if you have given the lesson fifty times before you must still prepare it anew.

2. KNOW YOUR SUBJECT: KNOW YOUR DRILL: KNOW YOUR EQUIPMENT. If you don't you are almost sure to be caught out, and your use as an instructor will go down. Know more than you propose to teach your class. With too narrow a margin you may find yourself on the edge of a precipice.

3. BE SIMPLE : BE LOGICAL : BE LUCID. You cannot be too clear in bringing out your lesson. Simplicity must be the key-note of all instruction.

4. BE ACCURATE : BE THOROUGH : BE PATIENT. Do not take it for granted that all you have said has been understood. Find out for yourself by questions. If the answers which you get are wrong it is probably your fault.

5. EXACT A HIGH STANDARD OF DISCIPLINE. From yourself as an example to your men—from your men towards you and their work.

6. MAKE EACH MAN FEEL THAT YOU ARE TEACHING HIM. If he does not then he will stop listening or attending and you will find that you have left gaps in his knowledge.

7. DO NOT CONCENTRATE ON ONE MAN : DO NOT ALLOW YOURSELF TO DISCRIMINATE OBVIOUSLY BETWEEN THE GOOD AND THE BAD. Everybody must feel that he has a personal share in the lesson, and everybody must have his proper share.

8. BE SURE THAT EVERYBODY CAN BOTH SEE AND HEAR WHAT IS GOING ON. Do not be content to accept their word for it. Make sure for yourself.

9. WHENEVER YOU CAN, PROVE YOUR POINT BY DEMONSTRATION. The brain most easily records what the eye has seen.

10. MAKE SURE ONE STAGE IS REALLY UNDERSTOOD BEFORE GOING ON TO THE NEXT. Look out for those gaps in knowledge. They are dangerous.

11. PRESS FOR QUESTIONS FROM YOUR CLASS. They will show how much the class has understood.

12. NEVER MAKE A MAN FEEL A FOOL. He will be quite ready enough to do so without your help, and he will only get discouraged.

13. DON'T SHOW OFF : DON'T BLUFF : REMEMBER THE TIME WHEN YOU TOO KNEW NOTHING. If you get caught out admit it. No one really admires the man who is too clever. Be honest with yourself and with your class.

14. LOOK YOUR CLASS IN THE EYE : ALWAYS TALK DIRECT TO THEM. You can only do this if you are confident in yourself. Only by that can you gain the confidence of your class.

15. **Avoid Tricks : Avoid Mannerisms : Avoid Distractions.**
These are the things which carry away the attention of a class.

Finally remember that the test of good instruction is not "Have I covered the ground ?" but "Does the other fellow know what I have taught him ?" Second rate or "slap-dash" instruction may lead to some disaster on the field of battle. If your men had been better taught vital mistakes might not have been made. You are fighting the enemy long before you get near the battlefield. But he will still be quick to take advantage of your mistakes. The finest equipment in the world is useless in the hands of badly trained men.

MAKE UP YOUR MIND THAT IT WILL NOT BE YOUR FAULT IF IT HAPPENS.

INFORMATION

THE OBJECT.

The object of the Information Room is to tell the soldier about the war in terms which he can understand.

The more a soldier knows, the better equipped he is to deal with his enemy. Under conditions of mechanised warfare, neither the training manuals nor the discipline which training engenders, are sufficient to produce the complete fighting man. He needs background, and particularly the background provided by maps, pictures and diagrams ; for the eye is a keener and surer avenue of intelligence than the ear. Moreover, it is often easier to learn under conditions of relaxation than under the tension of parades or classes. The Information Room, therefore, should be where the soldier takes his ease, and learns the background of his business, not because he is forced to learn, but because attractive presentations arouse his curiosity and make his lessons easy.

THE ROOM.

The first important thing to remember about Information Rooms is that they can be anything, anywhere. They need not be rooms at all. Just as a camp can be pitched on any site, so the Information Room can be constructed out of whatever materials are to hand. In the plains, a tent, hessian panels and durries on the floor will give you your Information Room ; in the jungle, bamboo will supply everything that you need. Please do not think of the Information Room, therefore, as something difficult or intricate to create. All you need is a little ingenuity and a few willing hands.

The perfect Information Room of course would be the "quiet room" of a soldier's club, where it would adjoin the recreation room or canteen. But under Indian conditions, and particularly under operational conditions, such accommodation is rarely available. Next best would be in recreation rooms themselves....a quiet corner. If the Information Room is elsewhere, it should be as near as possible to the recreation rooms or canteens ; or if not near, on the road or path to such centres. In the latter instance, a large bright sign should advertise the Information Room. It is important to begin with the psychological advantage of making a visit to the Information Room a part of a soldier's leisure—a place he visits because he wants to, and not because he must.

If a room is available, a floor space of 720 square feet (30' x 24') or upwards will suffice for the ordinary unit. Commensurate wall space should be available. When rooms are not available, and a tent is used, the lack of walls must be met by the supply of frames for the display of maps and posters. These frames can be built easily from hessian

ROOMS

and wood battens, and for operational units they can be so made that they will collapse for carriage. As to furnishings, these can be as elaborate or as simple as taste or necessity dictates. Tables (trestles) and chairs for British troops, durries and sitting space for Indian troops, are necessities ; other furniture is optional.

The first greatest necessity of any Information Room is illumination, Remember you are dealing with visitors whose interest must be aroused. Dim corners and ill-lit displays mean strained eyes and brain fatigue. You cannot have too much light in an Information Room. The Room really should be assembled around the available lighting facilities.

THE INFORMATION.

For the books, pictures, posters, diagrams, magazines, maps, broadcasts, and other information media which stock the Information Room, there are two prime requirements.

(1) **Keep the Material Fresh**:—The Information Room is not a museum. It only functions when it keeps up with the times. If a commander can hear his men say, "Let's drop into the Information Room and see what is new", he will know that it is a success.

(2) **Keep the Room Well-dressed**:—Information can always sell itself by intelligent display. Your graphic material—posters, pictures, maps and diagrams—will make or mar your Information Room. They are your window-dressers bait—to sell the goods which are on your shelves. Pictures should compel visitors to seek the story behind them. Maps should send men to listen to the radio. Daily news should send men to the maps.

MAPS.

Maps are the nerve centre of the Information Room. You cannot have too many of them, nor can they be too varied in type. • The chief map should be a large scale reference map of the world. Flags or chinagraph should mark the daily situation. Tapes should lead to pictures, explanatory clippings, or other items of interest, pinned on the edges of the map board. Slips of paper which state where reference material may be found, may also be pinned up. For a display plan for your principal map, see diagram at the end of this article.

Individual maps of the principal operational theatres—Russia, Italy, Burma, the South Seas, etc.,—should flank the main map. It is all one war that we are fighting, and every soldier should understand this.

DIAGRAMMATIC DISPLAY.

At the end of this article you will see a diagram which illustrates tie up between maps, pictures and news clippings ; this is designed to obtain a maximum impact upon the minds of soldiers. You will notice that the plan is designed to bring home the idea of global war and that everywhere we are on the offensive. The news cuttings and the picture sequences follow the events of the day, and should be altered as often as the supply of Information Room material permits. Fresh news cuttings usually are obtainable and should be renewed regularly. The picture sequence should be changed as often as possible, being replaced ι o fresh pictures are available) with picture clippings.

THE PICTURE SEQUENCE.

If you put pictures of a battleship, a camel, and a Jap, next to each other, you have no story—nothing but a mess, and wasted effort. To obtain an impact, pictures should be arranged so that a story flows through them, and so that there is a "carry over" of interest throughout the series. As illustration let us take one picture series in the diagram. Here are suggested sequences : (Figures given as Picture Numbers) :— R. A. F. OVER GERMANY—(1) Bombing Up. (2) Take Off. (3) Interior of Bomber in Flight. (4) The Bombs Go Down. (5) Bomb Bursts. (6) Ground Photograph of Bombs Bursting. (7) Post-Photograph of Damage. (8) Intelligence Check-Up on Bombers' Return.

Now it is unlikely that at any one time any Information Room would possess the eight pictures which complete this sequence. But this can be overcome by captioning. Thus if pictures (2) and (3) are not available, the captions on pictures (1) and (4) must be expanded to cover the gap. (Caption one : "Bombing Up for the Take-Off". Caption four : "After a Long Flight the Bombs Go Down"). Thus pictures and captions between them tell a coherent story.

When there are not sufficient or the right pictures to form picture sequences, there are other treatments possible. Some Information Rooms display pictures with the captions covered by a flap so that the observer must work out the story of the picture before checking his impressions with the caption. Others use a single picture as a tie up with news clippings. Pictures of towns, landscapes, etc. can be tied up directly into the map. Pictures in one sequence can be tied into another. (Thus "R.A.F. Over Germany" with "R.A.F. Over Italy".)

LITERATURE.

Keep your literature alive by a check list. If your periodicals are not up-to-date, find out why. The Director of Public Relations and the Director of Welfare and Amenities can supply you with a considerable list of publications. Put in an order for them. Unless you have the latest "gen", you are behind the times. Never be afraid to ask Public Relations or Welfare and Amenities for any additional literature which you may require. You may not get it, but both the foregoing Branches of G.H.Q. will supply your requirements if it is humanly possible to do so.

FILES.

The essence of Information Room organisation is that the material should be easily accessible. The best method of collating and storing

1. INFORMATION ROOM: THE INVITATION   *(To face page 48)*

    Note the cheerful sign in two languages, the planting
of shrubs to make the building attractive, the matting
and thatch construction.

2. THE MAP IS THE NERVE CENTRE

    An oversize map serves as the basis of organization
for this Information Room.

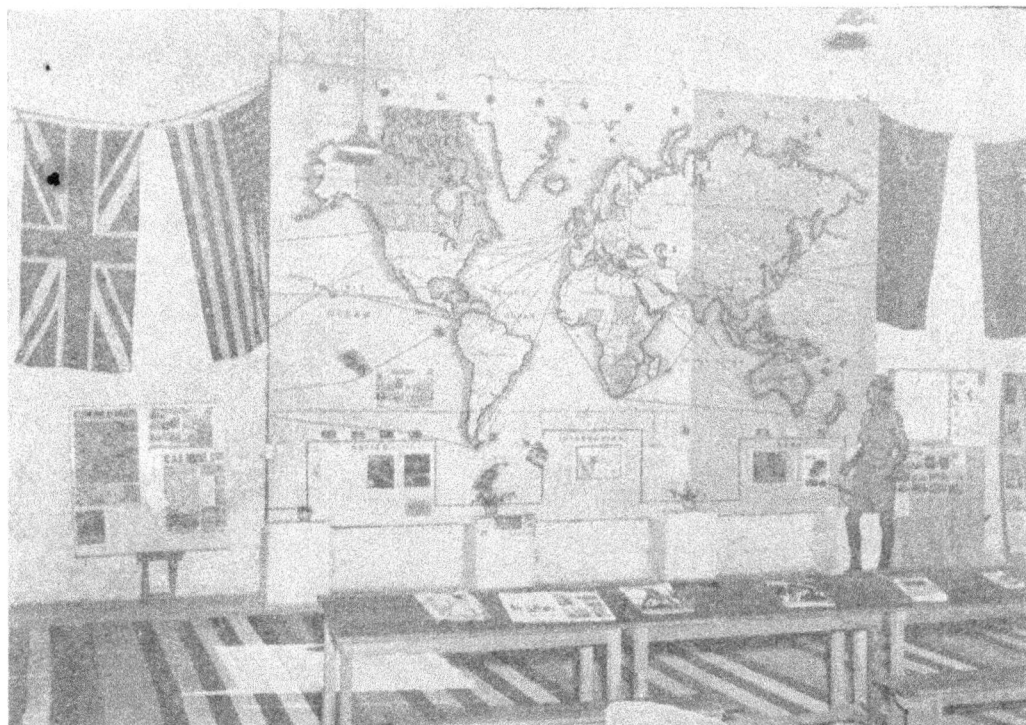

3. PICTURE TIE-UPS

This picture group is built around one subject—aircraft identification. All pictures are linked in this single theme.

4. MAP TIE-UPS

Note the tapes running from the world map to the detailed map, and from the detailed map to the reference book. Note also how well matting serves as a wall.

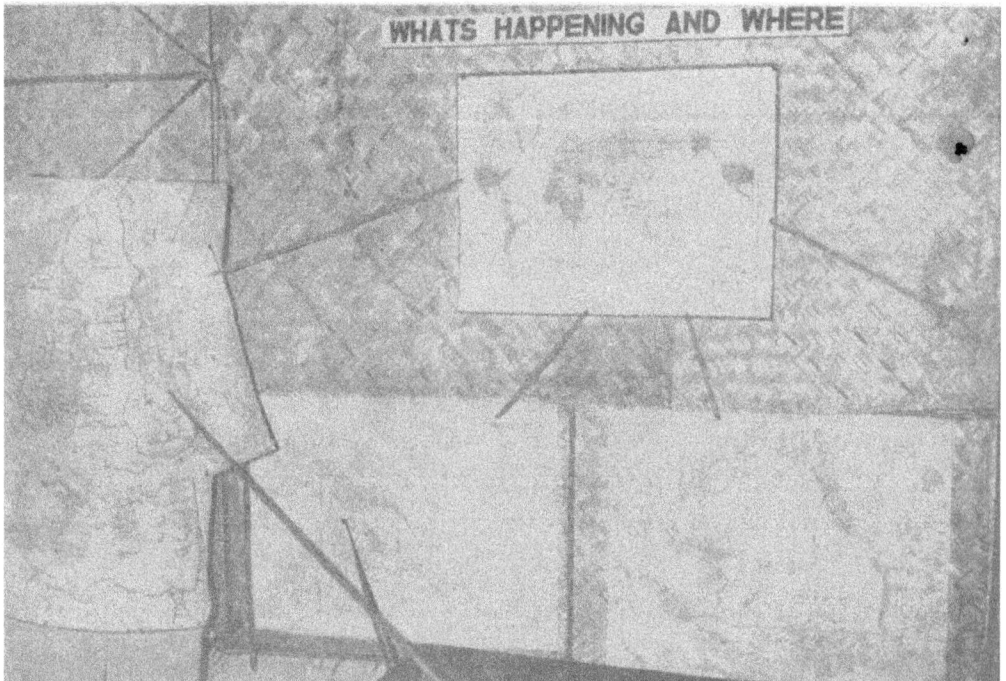

5. KNOW YOUR ENEMY
Note that the illustrations are life-size, and as near
as possible to eye height—an important point.

6. STUDY CHARTS
Aircraft identificaion is simplified by clever and
interesting study charts surrounded by action pictures and enemy weapons.

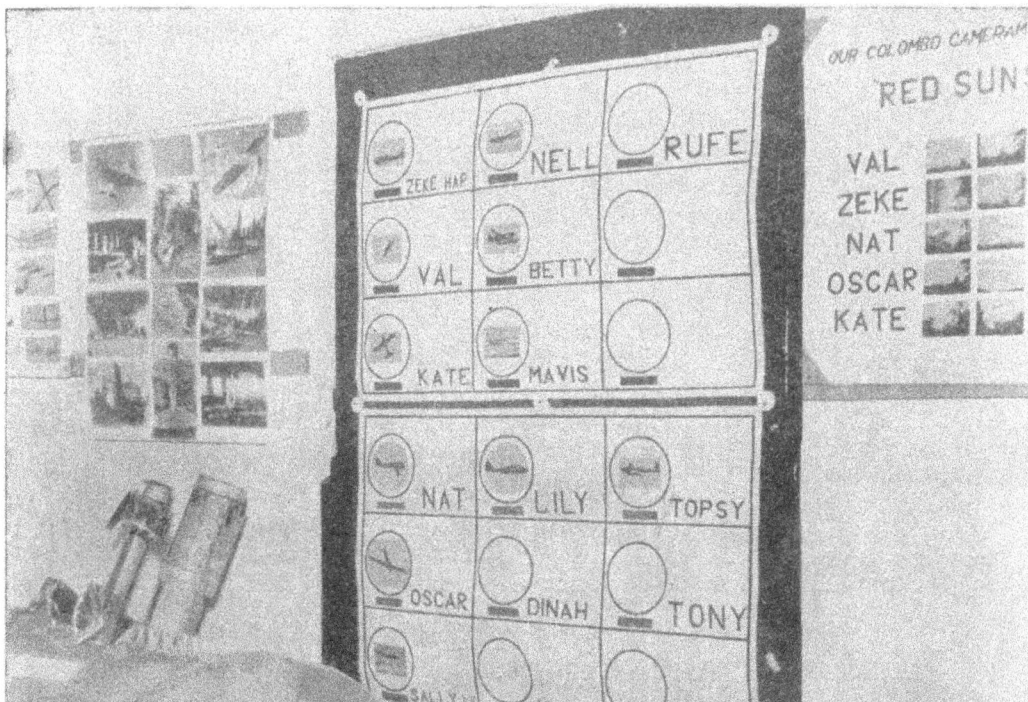

7. SUBJECT FILES
Picture sequences are pasted into a home-made
album for reference purposes

(To face page 49)

8. THE MUSEUM
A simple trestle construction supplies an excellent
museum display in a limited space. Note the ideas
box on the right, and the attractive posters on the
walls around the display.

information is in subject files. These files can be classified chronologically, by periods or seasons, or geographically—Russian Front, Italian Front, South Pacific Front—or they can be Service—Army, Navy, Air Force,—or they can be Informational, Weapons, Morale, Politics and so on. But you should not mix the various classes of files unless you have facilities for cross-indexing.

Very acceptable files can be manufactured with paste from brown paper. A list of files should be tacked on the notice board, and small tabs should be prepared for the mapping tapes. ("See File......for more about this subject").

NOTICE BOARDS.

A notice board is essential as a guide to the informational material. A blackboard (if available) makes a first class notice board. The new arrivals....maps, posters, literature... should always be advertised on the notice board. General enquiries ("Have you looked up the situation in the Southern Pacific lately") will serve to give visitors a direction in their research. Keep the notice board lively....it is your principal shop window.

MUSEUM.

For Indian troops. in particular, models and actual trophies have a most stimulating effect. Displays of weapons, plasticine or sand relief maps, enemy uniforms, and many other items have a distinct value in keeping the sepoy up-to-date with his war. But a museum corner in an Information Room is worse than useless if it is simply a heap of unassorted junk. Effective display is the key to success, and the problem of correlating museum exhibits is the same problem as building pictures into a picture sequence. A continuous story must be told. Isolated exhibits have little value.

A further word of warning about museums. Don't overcrowd your space. If something new comes in, throw out something old. The museum section of any Information Room should be under the control of the unit intelligence officer, who should supervise exhibits, and should be present on stated occasions to explain their implications.

ENTERTAINMENT.

Information is more easily assimilated through entertainment media than in any other form. This accounts for the great success of radio spelling matches, Brain Trust sessions and similar occasions in which the spectators have fun and instruction at the same time. Inter-company quizes and competitions, if properly organised (with officers taking part, and a few acceptable japes "planted" with members of the audience) make an evening pass very acceptably ; and an astonishing amount of information will be taken home.

SECURITY

The Information Room is designed to let the ordinary soldier know as much as possible about his war. This makes him a better soldier, but it also makes him a bigger risk. British and Indian troops are by no means as security-minded as let us say the Russians and the Japs; so allied to instruction there should be security reminders in the Information Room. **"Learn everything you can: and keep it all to yourself"**, makes a first class motto for any Information Room.

FINALLY.......

The Information Room can be a great factor in keeping your unit happy and in making your men better soldiers. But it will only yield in proportion to what is put into it. If the care of the Information Room remains one of the units odd jobs, results will be nil. **But take a pride in it, put some elbow grease and some headwork into it and it will play its part in getting this job over and in getting us all home again.**

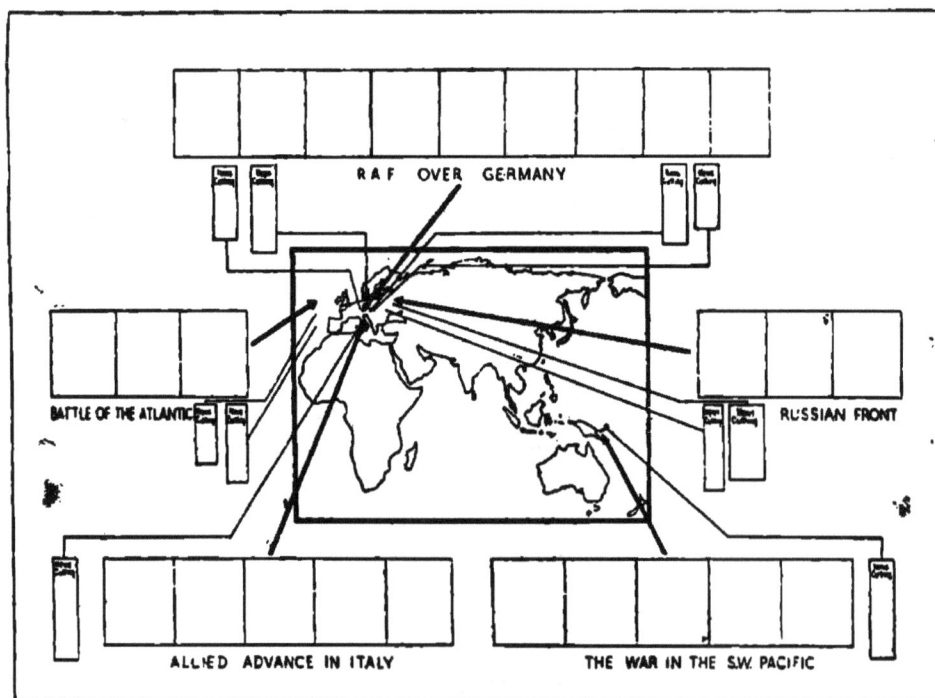

RAF OVER GERMANY

BATTLE OF THE ATLANTIC

RUSSIAN FRONT

ALLIED ADVANCE IN ITALY

THE WAR IN THE S.W. PACIFIC

The chart shows how a general map, the nerve centre of an Information Room, can be tied into the general news of the day. On the particular day illustrated on the chart, all fronts are represented. Five picture sequences and ten news cuttings carry the story of the war. The tapes and arrows are the connecting links.

PART TWO
USEFUL THINGS TO KNOW

14. BATTLE SWIMMING AND CROSSING RIVERS

That all soldiers should be able to swim is an ideal which has been repeatedly stressed. Recent operations have proved, if proof were needed, that even a non-swimmer must be able to cross water obstacles, confidently and quietly.

A non-swimmer will need the assistance of improvised equipment to keep himself afloat and, in certain circumstances, the help of a strong swimmer. So that a sub-unit can cross rivers and streams without delay, its commander should know the capabilities of each man and should see that those who can swim are detailed to help those who cannot.

Wherever suitable facilities exist, non-swimmers must be taught to swim, and swimmers urged to become more proficient so that the unit to which they belong will not be hampered in its movement across country.

Details of battle swimming and improvised methods of crossing rivers are published below :

BREAST STROKE

1. This is the most practical stroke. Its advantages are : —

    (a) Easy to teach to large numbers simultaneously. Instructions for teaching it can be found on page 38 of the handbook "Purposeful and Basic Physical Training 1942".

    (b) Conserves the swimmer's energy, especially when he is equipped in battle order.

    (c) The swimmer's head is out of the water and he can see normally.

    (d) It is the only really silent stroke.

IMPROVISED AIDS FOR WEAK SWIMMERS AND NON-SWIMMERS.

2. Materials most likely to be available are :—

    (a) Empty tins or boxes. Slow flowing water can be crossed by holding a box or tin to the chest with both arms and kicking with the legs. An empty petrol tin or .303 ammunition box will help to keep one man afloat.

    (b) Grass or straw, with which to stuff the gas proof cape into a bundle 2 feet 6 inches long by 1 foot wide by 6 inches deep. Use in the same way as tins or boxes.

    (c) Logs. These vary in buoyancy. Men should be arranged alternately on each side facing the far bank and be equally spaced. One arm should be placed on top of the log.

    (d) Trousers inflated and used as water wings.

3. An additional aid for use under more difficult conditions than those given above can be made by joining two boxes or tins together with rope or equipment straps. These should be used in the same way as water wings.

4. It is important to remember that these aids will not necessarily support the whole weight of the man. Weak swimmers and non-swimmers must be trained to allow the water to support their weight, only using these aids as an additional assistance. Provided a man keeps his shoulders below the surface and breathes normally, he will be buoyant.

IMPROVISED RAFTS AND BOATS.

5. Three devices are suggested. Each will carry a fully equipped man. Method (c) will carry up to 300 lb.

    (a) Lash a stretcher to two inflated inner tubes.

    (b) Make a framework of light sticks approximately 6 feet by 4 feet. Lash each corner to two empty petrol tins. Place a stretcher on top.

    (c) A boat can be formed from a tarpaulin cover from a 15-cwt. truck, a stretcher, and suspension bars. The cover is folded inwards towards the centre and the stretcher placed upside down on top. The two suspension bars are fixed one at each end. The rope passes through the folded cover, which is then pulled tight from the sides. The tarpaulin is then folded up and lashed to the suspension bars to form the ends.

6. Of the above devices, (a) and (b) can either be towed by swimmers or paddled. (c) will probably need a rope at bow and stern for hauling across the water.

It was found from experience in BURMA that the distance a swimmer carrying a line can swim across a river is limited. The current catching the rope will prevent him from reaching the far side. Further, if the river is more than 30 yards wide, it may be impossible to get the ropes tight enough for use in the ways described below.

CROSSING BY THE AID OF ROPES.

Single horizontal rope.

7. Two methods—(a) On top. (b) Underneath.

    (a) On top—Lie on the rope, grasp it with both hands, arms straight. One knee bent and ankle resting on rope. To climb, pull with the hands and press with the ankle.

    (b) Crossing underneath—(Three ways):—
      (i) Hang from the rope by hands and feet, ankles crossed. Move hand over hand and drag the feet along the rope.
      (ii) Hang by the hands and knees. To climb, move opposite hands and feet simultaneously.
      (iii) Using hands only, hang by the hands. Move the hands alternately a few inches at a time. A pendulum swing of the legs will help the movement.

LIFE LINES

8. Rifle slings or toggle ropes fastened together make a suitable life-line. To cross, lie on the back in the water and move hand over hand on the line. Lines placed at intervals down stream may prevent men who are carried away by the current from being lost.

CROSSING ON PARALLEL ROPES (2 Feet apart).

9. (a) Hands and knees crawl, moving opposite hands and knees together.
   (b) Lie on the ropes, arms full stretch, knees bent. To climb, pull with the hands and press with the legs.
   (c) Lie on the ropes as in (b), pull with one hand and press with opposite leg alternatively (Leopard Crawl).

HAND AND FOOT BRIDGE.

10. Two ropes, one 6 feet above the other. Grasp the top rope and stand on the bottom rope, traverse sideways.

THREE ROPE BRIDGE.

11. Two parallel ropes about 2 feet apart used as hand rails and a third rope 3 feet lower on which to walk. To cross, turn the feet outward, lean the body forward, keep the arms straight ; to check swaying, force the arms sideways.

CLIMBING ROPE LADDERS—TWO METHODS.

12. (a) Grasp the ropes with arms at full stretch and stand with both feet on the same rung. To climb, move the feet climbing two rungs in three steps, followed by the hands one after the other moving to full arm stretch. Keep close in to the ladder.
    (b) From the side, grasp a rung with each hand, one immediately above the other. Similarly place each foot on a rung, one immediately above the other, feet turned outwards. To climb, move opposite hands and feet together. This method is best when men are wearing full equipment.

CLIMBING SCRAMBLING NETS.

13. The clumsy, unskilled climbing of untrained men will cause confusion and delay when many are climbing at the same time. Awkwardness wastes effort. The method suggested is quick and efficient.

Move hand over hand on one vertical rope, feet on the wooden rungs on either side of the same rope, opposite hands and feet move together.

SWIMMING IN CLOTHING AND EQUIPMENT.

14. Trained soldiers' physical efficiency tests require the soldier to swim 60 yards in fresh water or 100 yards in salt water, wearing a denim suit. Then to-remain afloat out of his depth for a period of 2 minutes ; they also require him to swim 20 yards fully clothed and equipped in battle order—boots attached to the rifle butt or slung round the neck.

To attain this standard graduated training is necessary, even for strong swimmers. The distance at first attempted should not be more than 20 yards. Five stages in training are suggested :—

1st Stage — Denim suit.

2nd Stage — Denim suit, boots and anklets.

3rd Stage — Denim suit, boots, anklets, and light equipment.

4th Stage — As for 3rd stage, plus small pack and steel helmet. The steel helmet is strapped to the shoulder.

5th Stage — Full battle order. The rifle is carried slung across the back resting on the small pack. The steel helmet is worn with the strap across the forehead or at the back of the head.

If worn under the chin there is a danger of the swimmer choking, should the steel helmet become waterlogged.

ENTERING WATER CLOTHED AND EQUIPPED.

Points to remember :

15. (a) Enter at water level. If this is not possible, jump in feet first. It is safer than diving in—it is practical and the entry is more easily controlled.

  (b) The jump is made with the body straight and the legs together.

  (c) If the swim is long and time permits, the boots should be removed and tied to the butt of the rifle. The driving force in swimming comes from the legs and if they are impeded by the weight of boots, fatigue may result.

  (d) To guard against possible injury the rifle is slung across the shoulder and held in position by pressing down firmly with the fork of the hand at the lower sling swivel.

  (e) The steel helmet is strapped to the shoulder and not worn on the head. The impact of the water may cause serious injury to the neck if the helmet is worn with the strap under the chin.

FLOATING OIL.

16. If floating or burning oil is encountered, swim under water. On emerging to breathe, wave the hands about vigorously to clear the water of oil. Take a quick breath and submerge again at once.

For those who find under water swimming difficult, swimming on the back will minimize the risk of swallowing oil and injury to the eyes.

NIGHT TRAINING.

17. Tactical surprise can be effected by undetected crossings at night. To ensure silence the following points should receive attention :—

  (a) Men should be trained to wade silently in shallow water.

  (b) To enter and leave deep water without a sound.

  (c) Diving or jumping in should be forbidden.

  (d) Breast stroke should be used throughout.

  (e) The importance of correct breathing should be stressed, incorrect breathing causes coughing through water entering the air passages.

It is advisable at first to rehearse the exercise in daylight ; at night men will be expected to act without loud spoken commands ; even whispered commands may have to be dispensed with. In early training, the strangeness of night swimming will slow down action and movement, and some men may lose direction. Only short distances in familiar surroundings should be attempted at first ; patience and caution as well as silence are essentials to success. It is well to remember that many men have been drowned close to the shore, because, believing themselves to be in their depth, they have stopped swimming. It is advisable to swim ashore rather than to walk.

Non-swimmers being assisted by instructors and by
rafts made from their kit wrapped in ground sheets.
(Jungle Training Centre, Canungra)

Non-swimmers and weak swimmers using bamboo poles to assist
them across a river. The poles are 12 to 15 feet long and about
3 inches in diameter. One end is held firmly between the legs, and
the arms are used for propulsion.

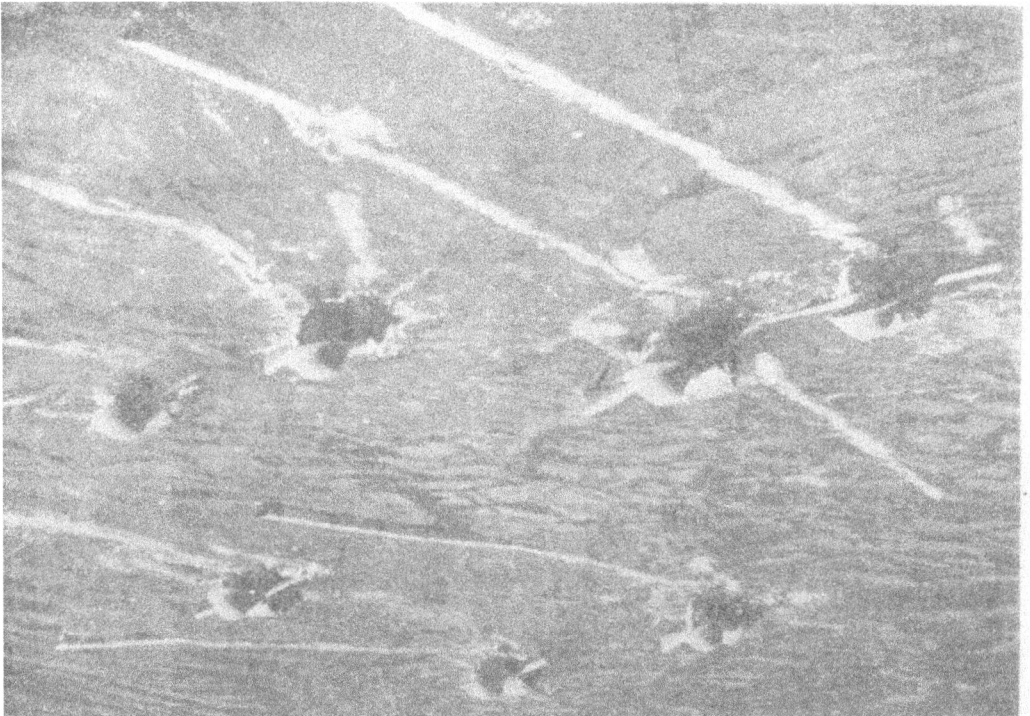

REALISM IN TRAINING

These photos were taken at the Jungle
Training Centre, Canungra, Australia.

(To face page 55)

15. RAFTING IN RIVER CROSSINGS

Recent operations in ITALY have emphasised the great importance of rafting in the opposed crossings of river obstacles. There will always be an interval of time between the assault across a river and the opening of the first bridge ; in the case of the VOLTURNO operation this was nearly four days. It is during this period that the provision of supporting weapons is so vital to the bridgehead force, yet a bridge at such an early stage is rarely possible and even if completed is liable to be bombed or shelled by enemy artillery as was the fate of a Bailey Bridge over the SANGRO. Reliance must then be placed upon rafts. They are less vulnerable than bridges, can be readily dispersed, and give flexibility to the commander's plan. Under certain conditions it may even be possible to connect the rafts together to make a bridge for night use only, to be split up again before daylight.

The value of thorough training and rehearsal was amply demonstrated at the VOLTURNO where previous practice in NORTH AFRICA contributed materially to success.

In future engineer training, stress will be laid on all forms of rafting particularly at night and with difficult approaches, and every opportunity will be taken to practise river crossing operations in co-operation with other arms.

Engineer officers and NCOs must be given practice in making river reconnaissance reports, as the success of the operation may depend on the accuracy and completeness of these.

When sufficient engineer personnel are available to carry out the complete reconnaissance, it will be better if the engineer officer commands the patrol, even though infantry may provide the escort.

This happy situation is, however, rarely the case in war, and it will be more normal for infantry patrols to provide the necessary information both negative and positive. Under such circumstances, whilst the infantry should know what the engineer wants, it will normally be advisable for an engineer officer to be present at the briefing of the patrols to ensure that no vital items are omitted from the patrol tasks.

———

16. HOW TO BLOW WEAPON PITS, 3-IN MORTAR AND 6-PR GUN PITS

After a successful attack, the infantry man is faced with the prospect of the delivery of an enemy counter-attack, preceded by heavy mortar fire, within half an hour of his arrival on the objective. In all the operations of this war, these counter-attacks have been delivered with monotonous regularity and remarkable efficiency.

During this half hour, if many casualties are to be avoided and the counter-attack driven off, the infantry men must find cover. The use of the enemy's pits is inadvisable, if it can be avoided, because he has a habit of registering them with his mortars before the attack is delivered and can bring down very accurate fire on them when required. And half an hour's digging will not provide very effective cover, especially in rocky ground. As a result of experiments, a method of using No. 75 grenades to blow pits has been devised. This method is still in the experimental stage but, since the grenades give a possible solution of this most important problem, details of results achieved to date are given below. It should be noted that pits blown in this way have soft sides and are not, therefore, proof against tanks.

General.

1. Experiments have been carried out on the hasty preparation of these works by the use of the No. 75 grenades. Results of the experiments are given below.

Method of Initiation.

2. The following methods of detonation can be used :—

(a) The 75 grenades are connected together by a length of primacord, FID, or cordtex to either a 75 grenade detonator or a No. 27 detonator. The detonator in turn is connected by a 2 min length of safety fuze with a chemical igniter (75 grenade) ; crushing the chemical igniter then fire the grenades. Sharp bends must be avoided in any of these types of detonating fuze, and the No. 27 or 75 grenade detonator must be arranged to point along the length of the detonating fuze. Otherwise the fuze is liable to be severed.

(b) Alternatively, cordtex wrapped completely round the body of the grenade once or twice has been found sufficient for detonation.

Two-Man Weapon Pit.

3. (a) Work to be done.

Spitlock shape 8 ft. by 4 ft. to a depth of 4 in. Dig two holes 1 ft. by 1 ft. 6 in. spaced 4 ft. apart. Place one 75 grenade in each hole, connect as described above, stamp down earth on each hole hard, and blow.

(b) Diagram.

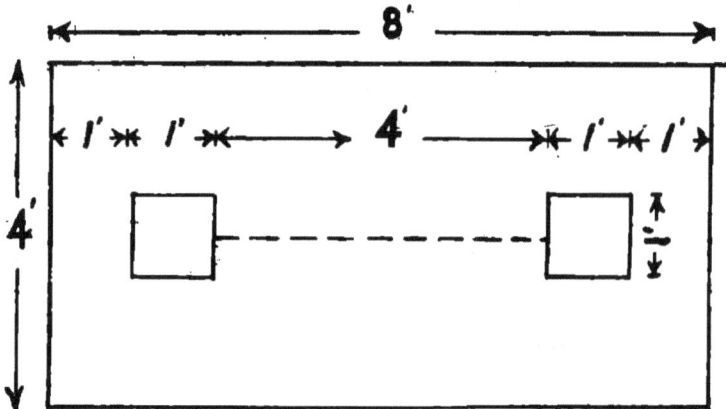

(c) Safety precautions.

Troops must be 20-30 yds. away from the slit during the explosion and wear steel helmets.

(d) Result.

A pit 8 ft by 4 ft. by 2 ft. 6 in. is blown and the earth is loosened sufficiently to dig out the pit to a depth of 3 ft. 6 in. with a shovel only.

(e) Time.

To prepare holes and grenades, and to
    spitlock the task   ....8 mins.
Digging out. ....10-12 mins.
Total time one pit, approx............ ...20 mins.
Pits for one platoon can be blown simultaneously.

3-in Mortar Pit or Coy. HQ Post.

4. (a) Work to be done.

Spitlock shape 10 ft. by 5 ft. to a depth of 4 in. Dig three holes 1 ft. by 1ft. by 2 ft. at 1 ft. 9 in. spacing and 2 ft. from the 10 ft. sides. Place two No. 75 grenades in each hole, connect grenades, stamp down the earth hard on each hole, and blow.

  (b) Diagram.

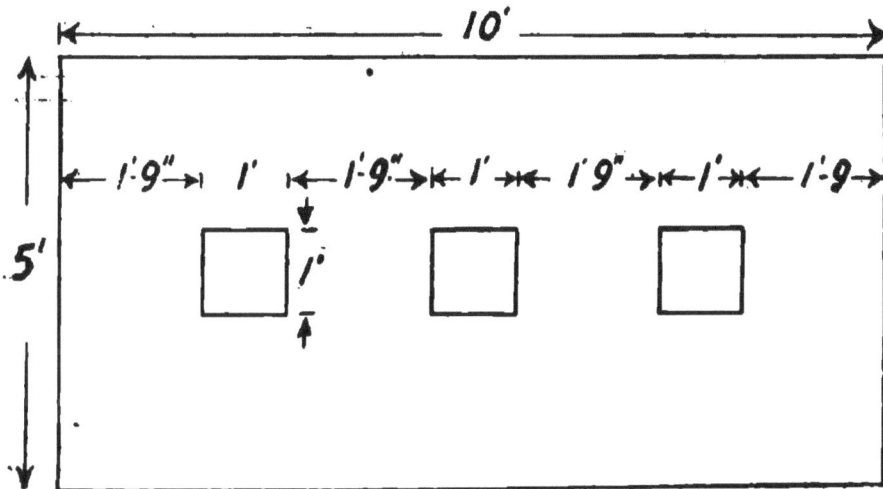

  (c) Safety precautions.

Troops must be 30-40 yds. away from the slit during the explosion and must wear steel helmets.

  (d) Result.

A pit 12 ft. by 6 ft. by 3 ft. 6 in. is blown and earth is loosened to a depth of 5 ft. and can be removed with a shovel.

  (e) Time.

To prepare holes and grenades, and to spitlock
    the task................................12 mins.
Digging out.......................................18 mins.
Total time, approx..............................30 mins.

N.B.—This normally is a 5 hrs. task for a 3″ mortar detachment.

6-pr Gun Pits.

5. (a) Work to be done.

Spitlock shape 6 ft. by 15 ft. by A as in diagram below.
Dig nine holes, each 1 ft. by 1 ft. and 1 ft. deep, arranged as shown in diagram. Place one 75 grenade in each hole, connect grenades, stamp down the earth hard, and blow.

(b) Diagram

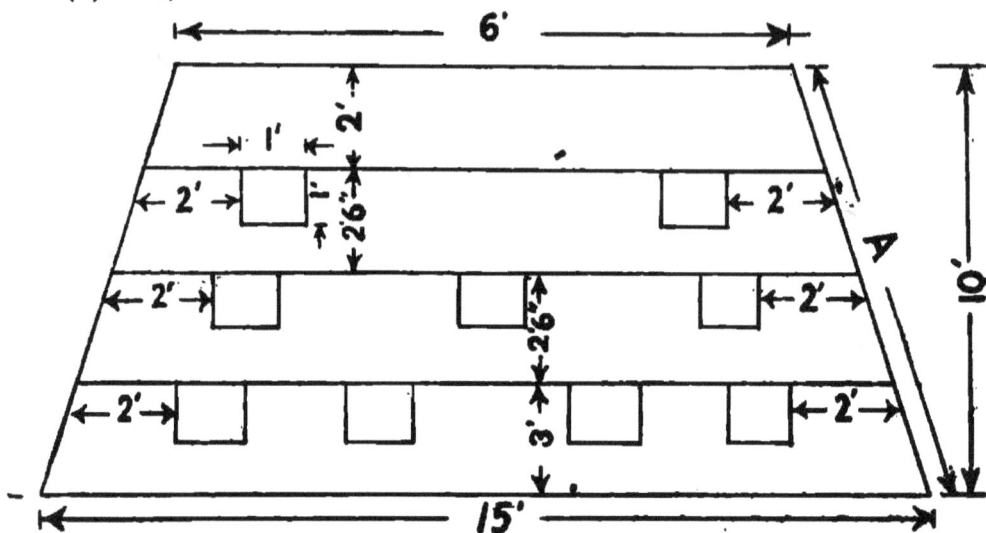

(c) Safety precautions.
Troops must be 30-40 yds. away from the slit during the explosion and must wear steel helmets.
(d) Result.
A pit shaped as in (b) above is blown to a depth of 2 ft. and earth is loosened to about 2 ft. 6 in. and can be removed with a shovel.
(e) Time.
To prepare holes, grenades and to spitlock the task..10-12 mins.
Digging out and manhandling 6 pr. into pit......10-12 mins.
Total time, approx.............................24-25 mins.

General Notes.
6. (a) Dimensions of the pits and the time taken to complete the work vary in each case according to the soil encountered.
(b) Spitlocking improves the results of the explosion.
(c) The cover provided is not tankproof, since the walls are soft and liable to collapse under weight.
(d) The narrowest and deepest crater is produced with grenades placed vertically as opposed to lying flat.
(e) A standard drill for constructing cover in this way is unnecessary. Care should be taken that the explosion of one lot of grenades does not interfere with the preparation of neighbouring pits.
(f) Similar trials using four 69 grenades connected together produced a two-man weapon pit of rather smaller dimensions than that produced by two 75 grenades. The use of 69 grenades is inadvisable for anything larger than a weapon pit.

17. MORTAR NOTE FROM NEW GUINEA

"One of the mortar sergeants," writes an officer, "has made a gadget which you fix to a 3″ or 2″ mortar, and by it you can tell if the mortar is going to fire through a gap in the trees or not. It works on the principle of the Vickers M. G. barrel inspection mirror, with a mirror looking up a tube parallel to the mortar barrel."

18.   WHAT HAPPENS TO THE BOFORS SHELL

The Bofors light A. A. shell is designed so that either it goes off on impact on the target, or explodes and destroys itself when it has passed its effective range.

The object of the self-destruction is to avoid the spent shell coming to the ground and causing casualties amongst our own troops.

That these facts are not understood by many is apparent from the commonly heard remark : "The bursts were miles beyond the enemy aircraft."

The following illustrations may explain the point :—

Phase I.

The moment that the shell passes the aircraft.

Assumed the shell missed the aircraft by 1″ and that the aircraft is travelling at 360 m. p. h. height 2000 feet.

Phase II.

The moment that the shell explodes.

The mathematics are approximate but sufficiently accurate for the purpose.

Heavy A. A. however uses a time fuze shell similar to shrapnel or air-burst and aims to burst the shell in the vicinity of the aircraft. In this case the criticism of shells bursting beyond the target is justified.

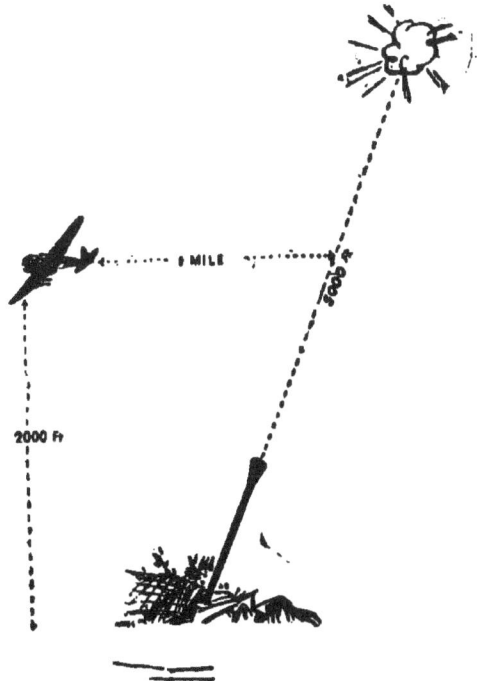

19. USES OF THE 75 GRENADE

Apart from its normal use as a mine, the 75 grenade is of value as a demolition charge. Here are two of its uses :—

   (a) A single grenade, when detonated, will cut a 90 pound rail if placed in close contact with it.

   (b) An improvised Bangalore torpedo can be made by lashing 18 grenades end to end on a wooden plank 11 ft. × 6 inches × 1 inch. A nineteenth grenade, exploded by a detonator and safety fuze, is used for initiation. This grenade is placed edge on to the end of the first grenade. All grenades must be fuzed.

   During tests, this torpedo proved to be less manœuvrable than the tubular torpedo. It was found difficult to push it through an obstacle wider than 10 feet. Apart from this limitation, its effectiveness has been proved. When placed at a height of 12 inches from the ground in an obstacle 14 feet wide, which consisted of two double apron fences with high concertina wire in between, the torpedo blew a clear gap of 15 feet in width and cut the screw pickets, with which it was in close proximity.

20. MAP REFERENCE CODES

There is some confusion over the use of the Map Reference Code and the Slidex R/T Code.

The Map Reference Code for general use is the "R. E. L. Code". It will be used for all map references transmitted in clear by any method except R/T which is liable to enemy interception.

Map references sent by R/T will be sent by SLIDEX R/T Code.

This does not affect the rule that map references of points readily identifiable by the enemy will not be encoded.

21. IMPROVISED TELEPHONES

Details of an improvised telephone used by units of the A. I. F. during operations in New Guinea, are shown in the accompanying figure. Simplicity in construction and the reduction in weight in no way affect the performance of these emergency telephones over comparatively short distances.

Details of their performance whilst under trial at the Army Signal School (India) are as follows :—

Satisfactory speech obtained :—

with 2 "S" cells over worn cable $3\frac{1}{2}$ miles.

  „ 2 "S" „ good cable 4 miles (minimum).

  „ 1 "S" cell worn cable 1 mile.

  „ 1 "S" „ „ good cable $1\frac{1}{2}$ miles.

An iron peg provides a more satisfactory earth connection and increases the range.

The absence of any calling device, such as a buzzer, excludes their installation on any line system working through a telephone exchange. They have, however, been used successfully with single cable, laid along jungle paths, providing intercommunication for sub-units of an advancing column. The operator of telephone connected to such a system calls up by means of speech using a pre-arranged code ; this necessitates the wearing of the headphones continuously by all telephone operators on the line.

LINE — L1. — TERMINAL BRASS

L2.

TO MICROPHONE

CORD SECURING
BATTERY

SINGLE 'S' CELL

PEG

TO HEADPHONES

EARTH CONNECTION
STICK INTO GROUND.

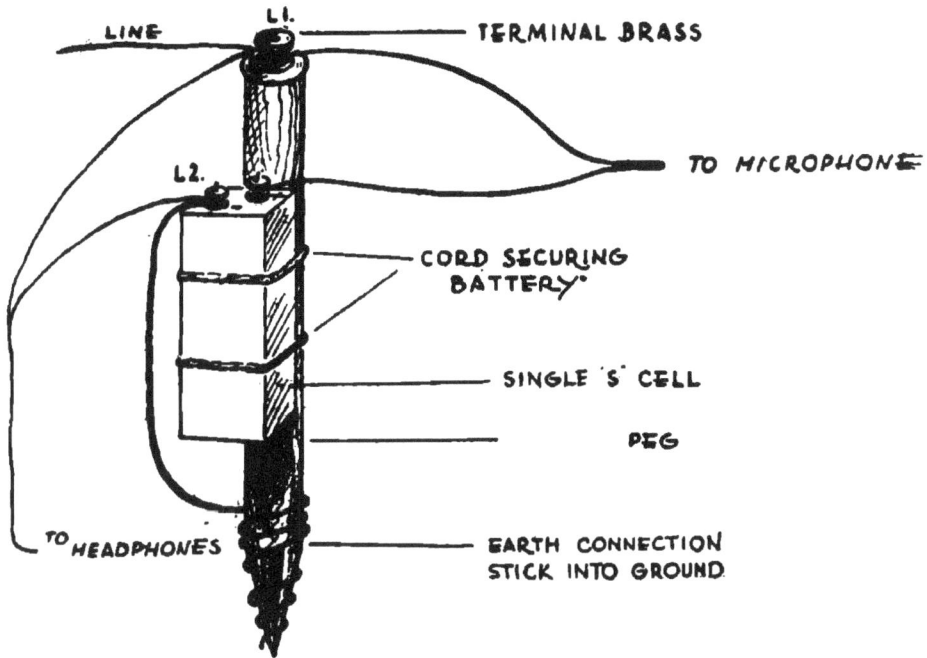

TELEPHONE CONN CTIONS USING WOODEN PEG.

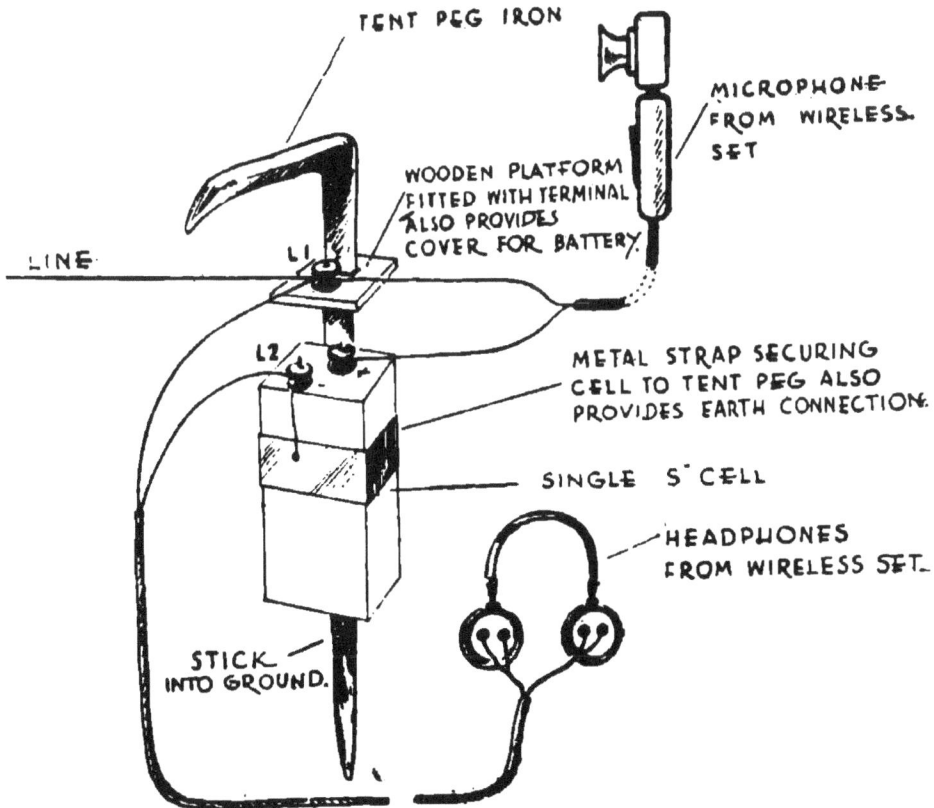

TENT PEG IRON

MICROPHONE
FROM WIRELESS
SET

WOODEN PLATFORM
FITTED WITH TERMINAL
ALSO PROVIDES
COVER FOR BATTERY.

LINE

L1.

L2.

METAL STRAP SECURING
CELL TO TENT PEG ALSO
PROVIDES EARTH CONNECTION.

SINGLE S' CELL

HEADPHONES
FROM WIRELESS SET.

STICK
INTO GROUND.

TELEPHONE CONNECTIONS USING IRON PEG.

22. TERMINOLOGY—"TRANSPORT BY AIR"

The following terms and definitions have been introduced to avoid confusion :—

(a) **Airborne**.

This term will be applied to all personnel who, normally forming part of airborne divisions, are specially trained and organised for operations involving transport by air. This term is applicable both to parachute troops and to airlanding units as well as to their equipment.

(b) **Air-transported**.

This term will be applied only to troops who are NOT a part of airborne divisions and who may be transported by air for a special purpose. The US Army uses the same phrase.

(c) **Air-portable**.

This term is applicable to the equipment, modified as necessary, that accompanies those troops who are air-transported.

23. LEECHES

One of the best ways of preventing the activities of the ubiquitous leech is to sew a piece of linen into the shape of a sock.

This linen sock may be worn under the ordinary sock. The most suitable cloth is that sold in the bazar under the name of "Latha".

24. AIR SUPPORT DEMAND FORMS

Reference Military Training Pamphlet No. 8 (India), Part II. Paras. 59 to 63 and Appendix "E".

1. A revised Air Support Demand Form for calling for air support has been brought into use within the India and South East Asia Commands.

The new form is shown on the next page.

2. The originator of the demand is responsible for completing Paras. B, C, E and F only.

Paras. A and D will normally be completed at the combined Army RAF Headquarters controlling the operation.

3. Military Training Pamphlet No. 8 (India) Part II is being amended accordingly.

———

AIR SUPPORT DEMAND FORM
(For use in India and S. E. Asia Commands only).

Air Force (Opl.) Form-906-8

From: (ARMY ONLY)		G R		Originators No	
To: (R A.F. ONLY)		G R		Ops. No:	

NO. OF AIRCRAFT required	**A**	
TARGET (To include any special purpose if not obvious in description of target)	**B**	
PREDICTED LINE OF FWD. TROOPS (Army only)	**C**	
BOMBLINE (R.A.F. only)	**D**	
SPECIAL INSTRUCTIONS (Time over target, position of indicator signs etc., if required)	**E**	
T.O.O.	**F**	SIGNATURE

SIGNALS USE ONLY	TIMES	OPERATOR	
T.H.I. TENTACLE			Not to be transmitted
T.O.R TENTACLE CONTROL			
T.H.I REAR LINK CONTROL			
T.O.R. REAR LINK			

REPLY TO DEMAND No. (In Code only)

ACCEPTED	**G**	
REJECTED	**H**	
NO. OF AIRCRAFT	**J**	
E.T.A.	**K**	
T.O.O.	**L**	SIGNATURE

25. ANTI-MALARIAL TRAINING.

IF....

If you can use intelligence and reason,
      When listening hard to what the doctors say,
And realise that in the rainy season,
      You have GOT to fight mosquitoes every day ;

If you can bear to hear the fools who chatter,
      (Of course, you know, I NEVER use a net !)
And tell you that it really doesn't matter,
      Yet still obey the orders that you get ;

If you believing others may be slacking,
      Can go and watch the doings of your men,
And finding that some discipline is lacking,
      Can give a talk about it there and then ;

If you will try to minimise infection,
      By thinking what to do about the drains,
And then ensure by personal inspection,
      That everything is right before the rains ;

If you will rub the ointment with your finger
      On portions of the body that are bare,
And when the evening cometh never linger,—
      For then it's time for trousers everywhere ;

If you can chide the other silly buffer,
      Who sits about with shorts above the knees,
And tell him what you think he ought to suffer,
      For giving chances to anopheles :

If you can bear in mind the orders given,
      And never stint that flitting with your gun,
Till all mosquitoes from your tent are driven,
      YOU'LL NEVER GET MALARIA, MY SON !

26. OPERATIONAL RESEARCH : WHAT IT MEANS AND WHAT IT DOES.

1. Officers commanding troops in the forward areas are so fully occupied in training their men, planning for battle, leading their men in battle, and looking after their men's welfare that they have little time to think out the lessons of battles they have just fought. Again, they cannot possibly know what science can do to help them to solve their day-to-day problems. And yet, if we are to keep ahead of the enemy, we have got to think not only of lessons of past battles ; we have got to think also in advance of means of defeating him in the battles about to take place, in the future, and we must make full use of all that science can give us in the process. The whole business of investigating future improvement and development is called Operational Research, and an organization exists for this purpose, the members of which have special opportunities for thinking about the future. As personnel of the organization will frequently come into contact with troops it is important that the latter should realize who they are and what they are for.

2. At present the Operational Research Organization in India consists of a small headquarters at G. H. Q. (the Research Directorate) with, working under it, an Operational Research Section (O.R.S.). This section comprises a small number of officers of different arms of the service, each one of whom possesses special qualifications for research work, including an Honours Degree in Science. These officers are normally located in the forward area, where they can collect facts at first hand. Many units will have already seen some of these officers in their areas.

Work of Operational Research Personnel.

3. The following are major items in the work undertaken by the Research Organization:—

(a) Investigating problems approved by the General Staff, and making recommendations for their solution. Some examples of past and present problems are given at the end of this article.

(b) Ensuring that the results of trials and experiments at Home are made known in the right quarters out here.

(c) When asked to do so, seeing that proper conclusions are drawn from experiments and trials.

(d) Ensuring that inventions and suggestions (many of which come from unit suggestion boxes) are examined by those best qualified to do so.

How the Research Organization Can Help Commanders.

4. Formation and unit commanders should take advantage of the presence in their area of any officer of the Research Organization. The following are some of the ways in which such officers can help :—

(a) Advice and assistance regarding the carrying out of user trials of equipment, weapons, etc.

(b) Collecting and investigating problems which commanders think worthy of investigation.

(c) Discussion with commanders regarding equipment and other matters in the light of special knowledge which may be at their disposal.

How Commanders and Troops Can Help the Research Organization.

5. The success of Operational Research is largely dependent on the co-operation of the fighting troops. Here are a few ways in which you can help officers from "Research" who visit you :—

(a) Give considered answers to all their questions, even if some of these may seem to you trivial and unimportant. They are not really so.

(b) Talk freely, hide nothing. This applies particularly if you are being questioned after a battle.

(c) Do not regard Research Officers as "spies". Their job is to help you and nothing else.

(d) Do not expect the information you give them to produce immediate results. Production and distribution take time.

(e) Finally, remember that what you tell them or what they see for themselves, while with you, may result in far-reaching decisions affecting the design of material (weapons, equipment, rations, medical stores, etc.) to be used by others in the future. So do your best for them as they will for you.

SOME EXAMPLES OF PROBLEMS UNDERTAKEN BY THE ORGANIZATION FOR OPERATIONAL RESEARCH.

1. What is the most suitable weapon for the Infantry Officer in Jungle Warfare ?

2. Is the present entrenching tool adequate ?

3. What is the maximum range required by 3-inch mortars ?

4. Is there a need for more 48 sets for use by FOOs and B. Cs.?

5. Is the present scale of outboard motors sufficient ? Prepare a specification of the ideal outboard motor.

6. Summarise the relative merits of different types of service bridge. How are these affected by tropical climates ?

7. Are the present methods of battery charging in the jungle the best ? If not, what is recommended ?

8. Analyse the causes of casualties with a view to discovering :—

(a) Means to reduce them.

(b) Which enemy weapons are proving the most effective.

9. Analyse the causes of failures in wireless sets. Can the present scale of holdings of spare parts be improved ?

27. PATROL ORDER CARD

Already being used by a division, this card is intended as a reminder to Patrol Commanders of the main points they have to cover in their orders before setting out.   It is printed pocket size.

1. Object of Patrol Task.

2. Information as to :—

    (a) Types of country to be traversed.

    (b) Enemy   (1) Strength.

                (2) Weapons.

                (3) Known position and patrol activities.

    (c) Own Tps. (1) Positions and strengths.

                (2) Patrol activities.

                (3) Artillery, M. M. G. and R.A.F. defensive and harassing fire tasks.

3. Plan for Carrying out Task.

    (a) Strength and composition of patrol.

    (b) Time of leaving and anticipated time of return.

    (c) Routes out and in.

    (d) Probable **Bounds.**

    (e) **Formation.**

    (f) **Dress** and camouflage.

    (g) Allotment and distribution among patrol of :—

           (1) Weapons.

           (2) Ammunition—S.A.A., Grenades, Explosives.

           (3) Rations.

           (4) Water and Sterilizing Tablets.

           (5) Medical Equipment.

4. Communications.

    (a) Outside patrol—by Wireless, Lamp, Verey Lights, etc., if any.

    (b) Within patrol—by **Special Signals.**

    (c) Passwords, if any.

5. Check up that all are clear on :—

    (a) All relevant items from paras. 1 to 4 above.

    (b) Action to be taken if at any time patrol is ambushed.

    (c) Necessity for avoiding leaving traces, e.g., litter, by which enemy can follow them up.

6. Check up that all members of the patrol have removed all

LETTERS and other MEANS OF IDENTIFICATION OR GIVING INFORMATION.

7. Put this card away with papers you yourself are leaving behind.

28. PATROL REPORT PROFORMA
(Used by a formation in BURMA)

1. Patrol commander_____

2. Composition of patrol_____

3. Orders to patrol before leaving_____
_____
_____
_____
_____

4. Time out_____

5. Time of return_____

6. Route followed_____

7. Enemy located or encountered

    at_____estimated strength_____time_____

    at_____estimated strength_____time_____

    at_____estimated strength_____time_____

    at_____estimated strength_____time_____

8. Casualties inflicted on enemy_____

9. Own casualties_____

10. Information from locals (giving time and place)_____
_____
_____

11. Ammunition expenditure_____

12. Losses of equipment or other articles_____

13. Brief topographical report_____
_____
_____
_____

14. General remarks on the patrol_____
_____
_____
_____

Signed_____
Patrol Commander.

15. Remarks by CO or IO_____
_____
_____
_____

29. THE ESSENTIAL QUALITIES OF A JUNIOR OFFICER

A senior officer commanding overseas considers the following attributes to be vital in the make-up of a company or platoon commander, if he is to lead his command with success in battle.

They are :—

(a) Speedy decision based on careful reconnaissance, and the capacity to take aggressive action without waiting to be told and without wasting time.

(b) A knowledge of manœuvre ; how to put in a quick flanking attack when it is required, and how to avoid throwing troops away by pounding straight ahead against well-organised resistance.

(c) A high standard of map reading, especially of foreign maps.

(d) An accurate knowledge of the use of the compass and of other aids to the maintenance of direction.

(e) Ability to handle his command at night in the approach march, forming up, night attack, silent approach, and bayonet assault.

(f) Capacity to reorganise on an objective.

———

30. "TAKING STOCK"

All ranks, of whatever arm or service, must be trained not only to do their jobs efficiently in their own sphere, but also to fight with their small arms if required to do so in an emergency.

Commanders of units whose primary role does not involve fighting with small arms should ask themselves two questions. First, will my unit function efficiently in its own particular role under active service conditions ? Secondly, if attacked by the enemy from the ground or the air, will all the men know what to do and will they be able to handle their ground and anti-aircraft weapons sufficiently well to kill the enemy ?

If the answer to each question is an honest "Yes", then the C.O. is to be congratulated because he has kept a firm balance between two greatly conflicting factors. If the answer to either question is less than an honest "Yes", then something must be done at once to put the matter right.

If a unit's specialist training is skimped, a whole formation may suffer. At the same time a unit's general battle training is likely to be tested as soon as it arrives in an operational theatre of war. For these reasons, the scales must be carefully balanced.

PART THREE
JUNGLE LANES
31. THE JUNGLE LANE TO TEACH JUNGLE LORE

The object of this Jungle Lane is to teach Jungle Lore, to show how Nature can be used in the Jungle, and to show our own and Jap methods of Jungle Craft.

The Lane, which is an ordinary track running through the jungle, can be of any length, depending upon the amount of Jungle Craft and Lore to be demonstrated. At the Jungle Warfare School, Shimoga, the Lane is approximately 750 yards in length. The Lane is made up of several demonstrations, which are shown one after the other. Each demonstration is then made the subject of a training period.

Points to be shown, are :—

(a) Correct use of light and shade and foliage, by patrols.
(b) Noise in close jungle.
(c) Sentries.
(d) Bird calls, cow bells, etc.
(e) Tree signs, Jap and our own.
(f) Booby traps, and bird snares. Grenades, panjis, spears, arrows, etc.
(g) Footprints.
(h) Leaves, and broken twigs.
(i) Snipers and false movement.
(j) Methods of cooking. Jap and our own.
(k) Shelters.
(l) Emplacements.

The Lane. (See sketch).

Phase I. Patrols. (a) Bad. Patrol moving carelessly on track. Weapons not ready. Pulling on branches of bushes, etc. Sound heard and patrol halts **on the track.**

(b) Good. Patrol using both sides of the track inside the jungle. Silence, and rifles correctly held. *Note.*—Explain to students that no patrol can be expected to get right up to a position without being seen, but a patrol can get near a position, before it is discovered.

Phase II. Noise. (a) Chopping wood.
(b) Singing.
(c) Whistling.
(d) Laughter.
(e) Combination of above. *Note.*—Explain that this is a happy patrol going into harbour, and that they are giving themselves away by their noise. The result is
(f) Jap attack signal. Gong.
(g) Jap attack. *Note.* The attack is made by two L. M. Gs. firing ball ammunition into a pit, and one Tommy Gun. Also four slabs of gun cotton. These are spread round the students, and just out of sight, to give the impression of being surrounded. Explain that noise of attack made by three men only.

THE JUNGLE LANE TO TEACH JUNGLE LORE

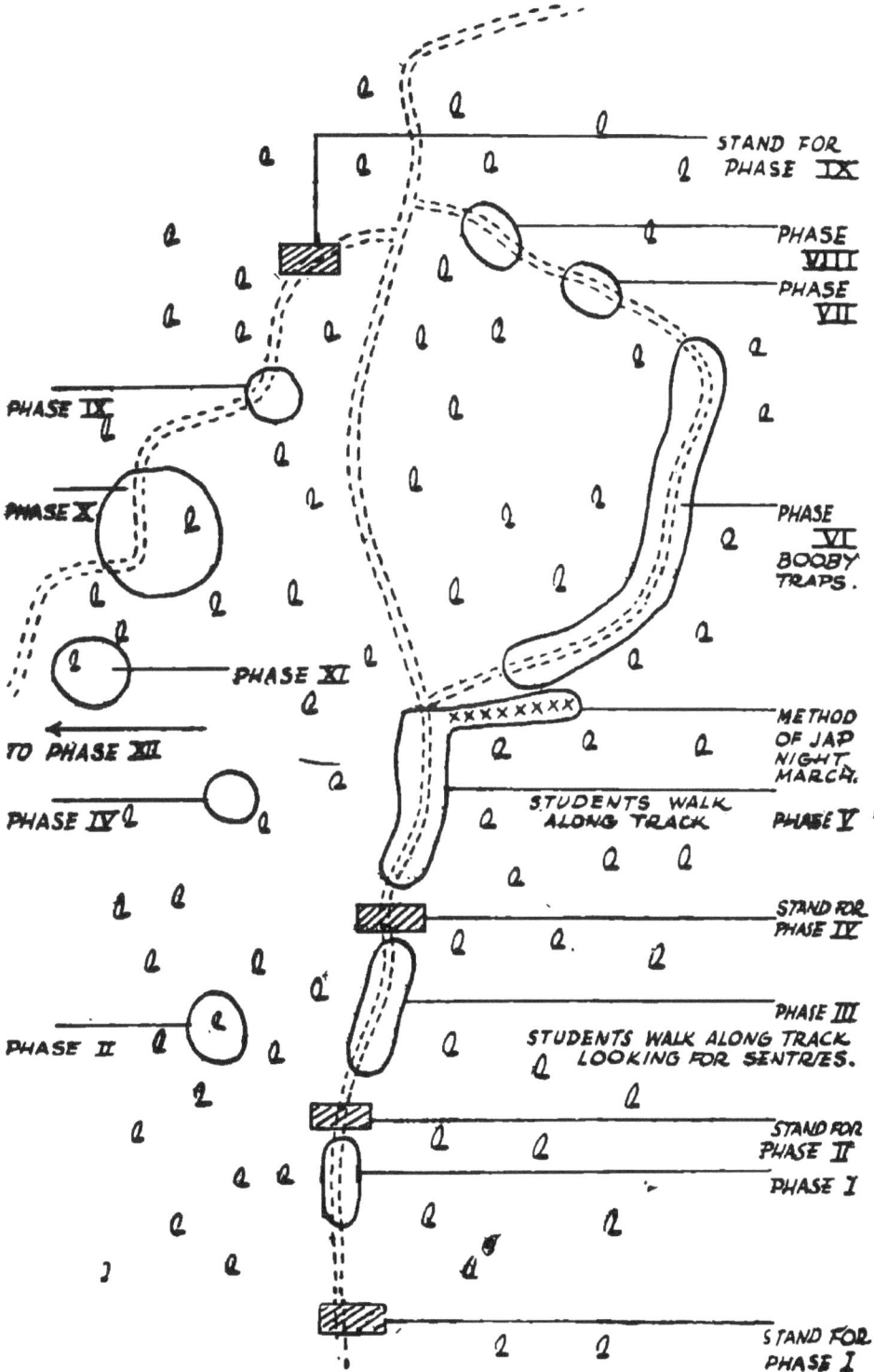

STAND FOR PHASE IX

PHASE VIII

PHASE VII

PHASE IX

PHASE X

PHASE XI

TO PHASE XII

PHASE IV

PHASE II

METHOD OF JAP NIGHT MARCH.

STUDENTS WALK ALONG TRACK — PHASE V

STAND FOR PHASE IV

PHASE III
STUDENTS WALK ALONG TRACK LOOKING FOR SENTRIES.

STAND FOR PHASE II

PHASE I

STAND FOR PHASE I

PHASE VI BOOBY TRAPS.

Phase III. Sentries. (a) Lying.
                   (b) Sitting.
                   (c) Standing.
                   (d) Tree sentry.

Note.—Explain that these are sentries, and NOT snipers. They have a string or creeper attached from their post to the section commander.

One tug means a local, two tugs means an enemy, etc. Must be very patient, and silent, carefully concealed, and prepared to remain in same position for hours.

Phase IV. Calls. (a) Bird calls.
                (b) Animal calls.
                (c) Woodpecker.
                (d) Frog.
                (e) Cow bell.

Note.—Explain that men are very shy at first, and cannot make calls, etc., but if a competition is held, many calls will be forthcoming.

Noise of woodpecker and frog, made with bamboo.

Phase V. Tree Signs. (a) Blazings on trees denoting passing of patrols, etc.
                (b) Blazing, denoting hidden message.
                (c) Arrow cut in ground.
                (d) Bent branches and twigs.
                (e) Jap method of marking night march.
                (f) Methods of blocking a path.
                (g) Cut wood on track denoting direction to be taken.

Phase VI. Booby traps. (a) Panjis pit.
                (b) Methods of using grenades.
                (c) Note book on track.
                (d) Rolled up shirt, containing grenade.
                (e) Falling stone.

Note.—Explain that falling stone with a panji, can be used for killing for meat.

                (f) Flying arrow.

Note.—Explain mechanism.

                (g) Flying spear. Two kinds.

Note.—Explain mechanism.

                (h) Panjis lane.
                (i) Bird snares.

Note.—Explain mechanism.

Phase VII. Footprints. (a) Boots. Ours and Jap.

Note.—Explain that Jap has got many of our boots, but has overnailed them.

                (b) Shoes. Ours and Jap.
                (c) Naked foot.
                (d) Jap "tabi".

Note.—Explain that if footprints are not visible, can often be made so, by carefully

	blowing on the ground, when dust will go, leaving the impression behind.

Phase VIII. Leaves.
 (a) Lane of teak leaves.
 (b) Lane of jungle litter.
 (c) Lane of dried bamboo leaf.
 (d) Lane of broken twigs.
 Note.—Walk over each lane in turn, and show that some leaves make more noise than others.

Phase IX. False Movement.
 Sniper fires, and at some time bush moves.
 Note.—Explain that just before sniper fires, confederate pulls string attached to bush. Bush moves, and hence eye attracted to that direction.

Phase X. Cooking.
 (a) Three stones.
 (b) Two trenches.
 (c) Horizontal bars with two forked sticks.
 (d) Three pegs.
 (e) Tin. Sand and petrol mixed.
 (f) Sand pit.
 (g) Pits cut in earth.
 (h) Containers, made from bamboo.
 Note.—Walls of bamboo should be shaved down to allow of quicker heating.
 (i) Plates. Cups. Spoons.
 (j) Headwear.
 (k) Lighting fire, without matches, using bamboo-friction.
 Note.—Explain that after food has been cooked *ALL* traces of area should be hidden, and no litter left behind.

Phase XI. Shelters.
 (a) Lean to. Made with one side only. Capable of taking three men.
 (b) Lean to. Made with two sides.
 (c) Dog kennel.
 Note.—Must have two exits.
 (d) Raised floor. Usually used for a prolonged stay, such as in stockade.
 Note.—Explain how long it takes to make each kind of shelter, and how many men employed.
 Explain that shelters will be made some distance away, and brought to present area. When patrol leaves area, shelters to be laid flat on ground, so that Jap patrol cannot see from a distance.

Phase XII. Emplacements.
 (a) M. M. G.
 (b) Patrol shelter.
 Note.—Explain that spoil must be removed to a distance.
 Connecting trenches to be covered over with branches, to prevent observation from air.
 Track discipline essential.

32. THE JUNGLE LANE FOR OBSERVATION TRAINING

1. The object of this Jungle Lane is to develop, by object lesson, the faculties of observation and recognition, by sight, sound and smell, of the troops. In addition it develops alertness and the suspicious mind.

2. The following are among the more important detailed lessons which can be taught by this lane :—

(a) The effect and meaning of certain noises in thick jungle.

(b) The effect of natural and artificial camouflage and its detection.

(c) Recognition of enemy equipment and methods, e.g., footprints, badges of rank, places of concealment, ruses.

(d) Detection and removal of booby traps.

(e) Action on discovery of the presence of enemy, or on being ambushed.

(f) Recognition of unusual natural phenomena, and their meaning whether caused by man or nature, and the memorising of such phenomena as "jungle sign posts" for future recognition of the locality.

3. The layout and method of use of a typical Jungle Lane is as follows. Take any path through jungle or other very close country, preferably a winding path with very limited visibility to either flank. A length of 200 to 400 yards according to the lessons to be taught is suitable.

On the path, or at varying distances to either side, place different "hazards". A large variety of these can be devised by the use of a little imagination, and should be used according to the standard of training of the troops being exercised, and to the object of the exercise. The following are among those in general use—Jap footprints ; camouflaged snipers in trees and undergrowth, or in hollowed out ant heaps ; enemy defensive positions ; noises of movement, twigs snapping or footsteps in a stony nala ; booby traps, including panjis concealed in grass ; half concealed "dead men", rifles, helmets, pull-throughs, etc.; smouldering fires ; broken branches, twigs and leaves, disturbed earth ; birds nests, animal spoor.

Men move through the lane in single file at intervals. They report their observations to the instructor at the far end, who then criticises by taking them along the lane pointing out the "hazards" and bringing home the lessons learnt.

4. This method of observation training should, of course, be applied progressively. In the early stages of this training only simple and easily seen "hazards" should be used, later increasing the difficulty by means of booby traps and the use of blank fire. An interesting exercise bringing out the application of intelligence to observation can be carried out when men are really practised. This is to plant evidence on the ground which tells the story of the actions of a Jap patrol, its strength in men, animals and weapons, intentions, direction of movement, and probable present whereabouts. Men should observe and deduce and if unsuccessful walk into an ambush staged for the purpose.

5. Lanes must continually be changed. This presents NO difficulty since they take very little time to prepare. It has been found most effective to arrange lanes without warning on the normal routes taken by troops to their places of parade. This has the effect of developing by continual practice the habit of observation and suspicion so essential to troops engaged in fighting, especially in the jungle.

6. A diagram is attached.

THE JUNGLE LANE FOR OBSERVATION TRAINING

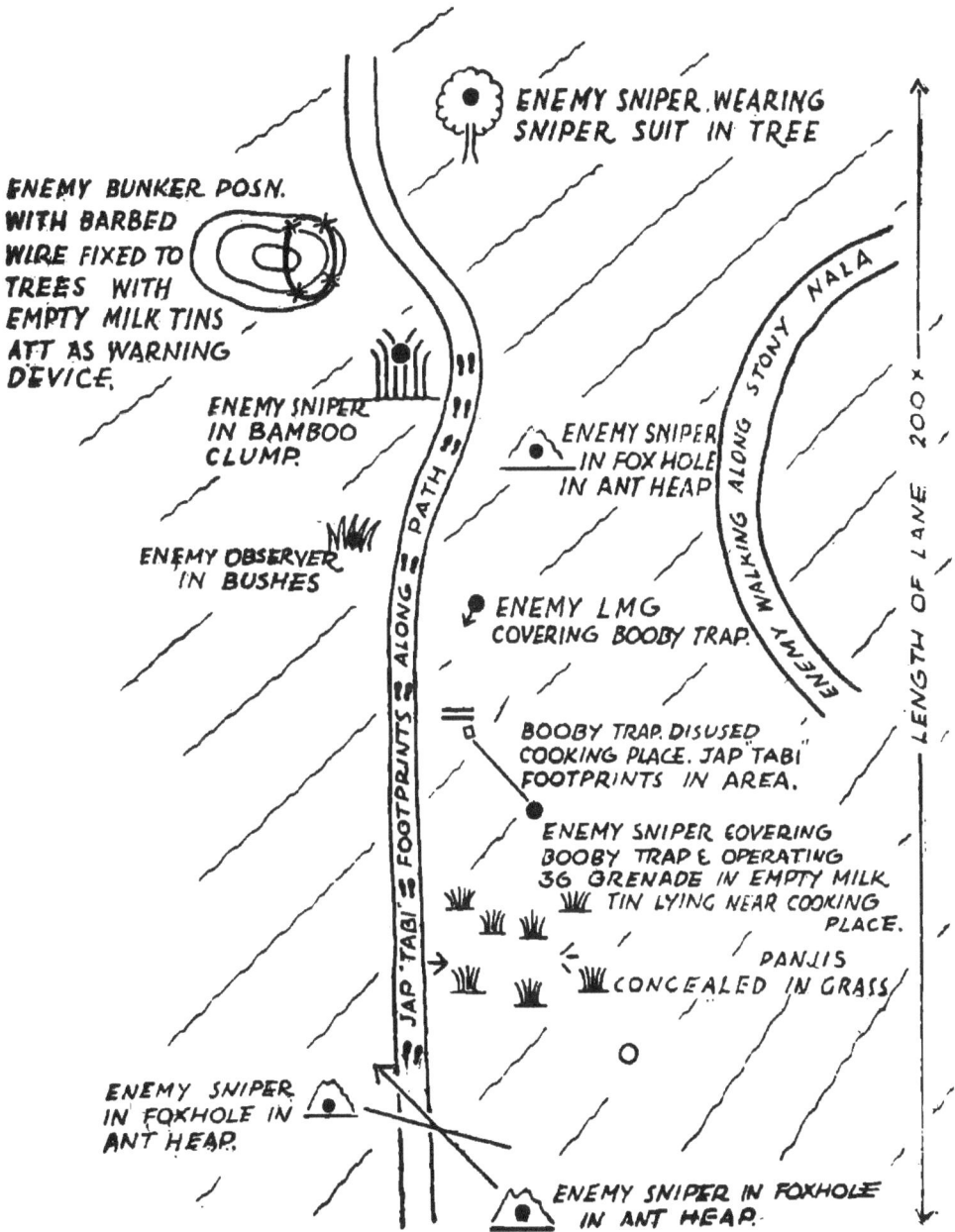

ENEMY SNIPER WEARING SNIPER SUIT IN TREE

ENEMY BUNKER POSN. WITH BARBED WIRE FIXED TO TREES WITH EMPTY MILK TINS ATT AS WARNING DEVICE.

ENEMY SNIPER IN BAMBOO CLUMP.

ENEMY OBSERVER IN BUSHES

ENEMY SNIPER IN FOX HOLE IN ANT HEAP

ENEMY WALKING ALONG STONY NALA

LENGTH OF LANE 200 x

ENEMY LMG COVERING BOOBY TRAP.

JAP TABI FOOTPRINTS ALONG PATH

BOOBY TRAP. DISUSED COOKING PLACE. JAP TABI FOOTPRINTS IN AREA.

ENEMY SNIPER COVERING BOOBY TRAP & OPERATING 36 GRENADE IN EMPTY MILK TIN LYING NEAR COOKING PLACE.

PANJIS CONCEALED IN GRASS

ENEMY SNIPER IN FOXHOLE IN ANT HEAP.

ENEMY SNIPER IN FOXHOLE IN ANT HEAP.

SKETCH OF A SNAPSHOOTING LANE

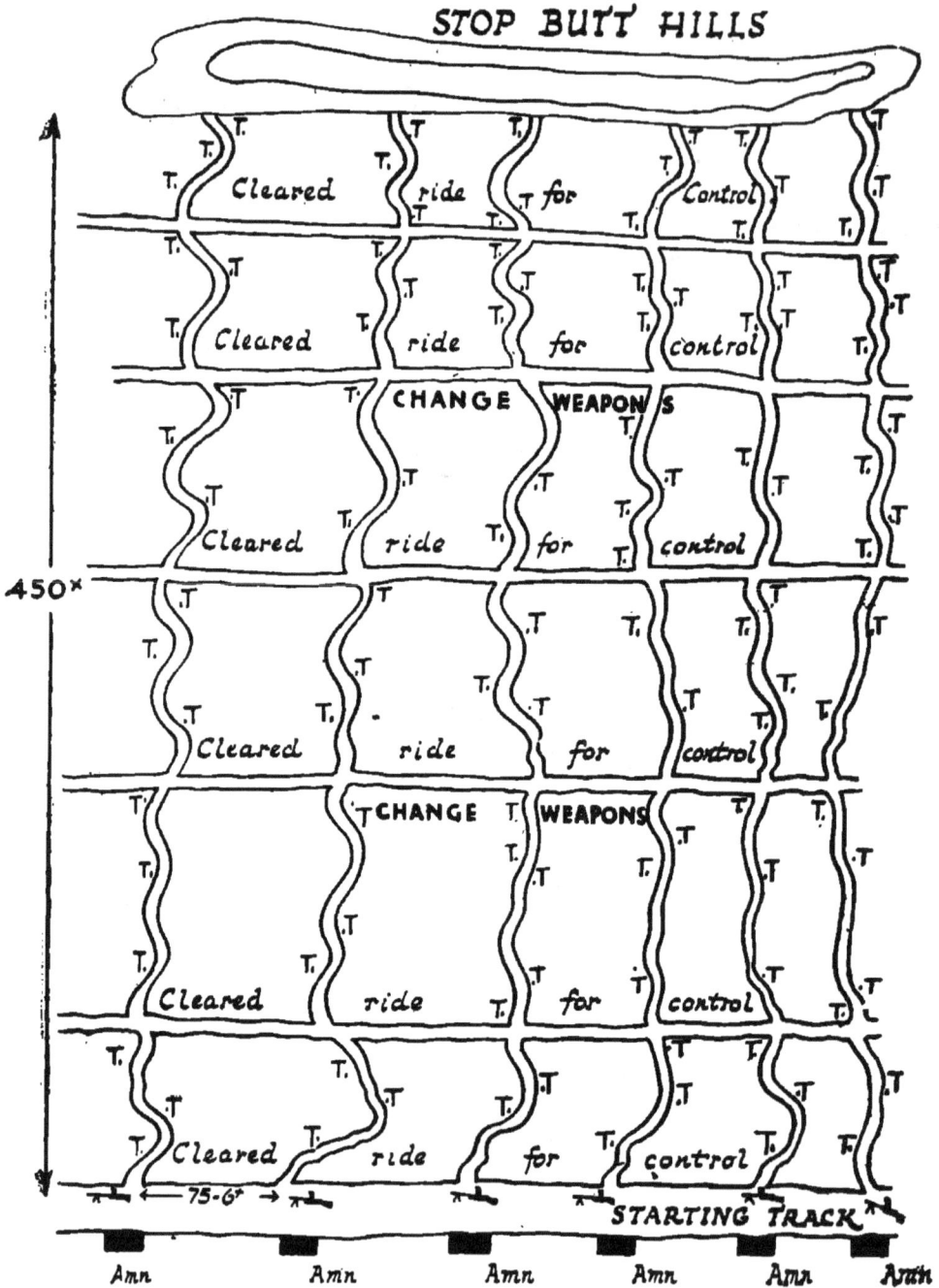

STOP BUTT HILLS

450ˣ

All Firers Start with L.M.G

Note: Country is intersected by steep nalas, thick scrub or jungle.
" T " indicates position of targets.

33.   A USEFUL JUNGLE SNAPSHOOTING LANE

1.   See rough sketch opposite.

2.   Details start together and move, each man down his own lane, controlled by an officer with a megaphone down one of the centre lanes. With each firer moves an instructor.

3.   All three section weapons are practised in each run, rifle, L.M.G. and T.S.M.G. The firer starts with one, changes after 150 yards and again after 300 yards, returning the weapons to their proper places as he comes back.

4.   Targets are small, at all angles and heights from the firer and in every case are come upon suddenly. If sufficient breakable chattis can be provided, all the better.

5.   All shooting is single shot. NOT more than two shots at any target.

34.   JUNGLE ARTS AND CRAFTS EXHIBITION.

A new application of the Jungle Lane idea, which for want of a better name may be called a Jungle Arts and Crafts Exhibition, is being carried out by a unit.

The object of this is to familiarise trainees on arrival with various aspects of jungle warfare so that they know what is coming to them from the start.

Various exhibits are laid out over an area, each one applied to the ground as it would be encountered in the field.

Trainees are taken from one to the other by their instructors, who describe them and encourage questions.

Exhibits are as follows :

(a) Organised defence position, consisting of a fully developed platoon locality in the jungle. It includes a bunker, weapon pits and one man keyholes, with communicating crawl trenches. It is camouflaged.

(b) Grass and bamboo lean-to shelters. Rope making machine. Bamboo expedients.

(c) River crossing expedients.

(d) Men in Jap uniforms. Footprints made by men wearing various footwear, also running and limping, including old and fresh prints.

(e) Pitfalls, panjis and booby traps.

(f) Hidden men demonstrating likely (and unlikely) places of concealment.

(g) A defended village, including demonstration of clearance.

(h) Bamboo stockade.

(i) Jungle cooking and edibles.

(j) Noises off.

This is an excellent idea to overcome the initial jungle shyness of the trainee, and to train him by eye to understand what is meant when references are made to these exhibits during the early stages of his jungle training.

Every point, whether tactical or administrative, should be brought out by instructors during the exhibition, and the maximum interest fostered.

Auchinleck

General

Commander-in-Chief in India.

APPENDIX A

LIST OF PUBLICATIONS

The following Training Publications and Amendments have been issued subsequent to those notified in A. I. T. M. No. 24—Appendix "E".

Serial No.	Publications.	I. A. O. notifying the issue.
1.	Combined Operations Pamphlet No. 35C—Transportation Units, 1943	249
2.	Artillery Training, Volume II, Pamphlet No. 16—Deployment of a Heavy Anti-Aircraft Regiment, 1943 ..	249
3.	Artillery Training, Volume II, Pamphlet No. 17—Deployment of a Light Anti-Aircraft Regiment, 1943 ..	249
4.	Instructions for Recording and Analysis—Anti-Aircraft Artillery (India)	249
5.	Roman Urdu Manual of Instruction on the Use of Homing Pigeons in India, 1943	249
6.	Combined Operations Signal Book, 1943	454
7.	Combined Operations Pamphlet No. 34—R. A. 1943 ..	454
8.	Small Arms Training Volume I, Pamphlet No. 14 (India), 1944—Range Courses, War	454
9.	Artillery Training Volume III—Field Gunnery, Pamphlet No. 5—The Employment of Base Ejection Smoke and Chemical Shell, 1943	454
10.	Gun Drill for 40-mm. A. A. Gun on S.P. Mounting (Modified for India), 1943	454
11.	Field Engineering Pamphlet No. 9—British Booby Traps, 1943	454
12.	Wireless Set No. 38 Mk. 2. Working Instructions ..	454
13.	First Aid on Active Service (English and Roman Urdu editions)	454
14.	What an Infantry Subaltern Really is	454
15.	Battle Bulletin No. 1—January, 1944	454
16.	The Hardening of Troops for War, February 1944 ..	454
17.	Army in India Training Memorandum No. 24 (War Series), March, 1944	659
18.	Combined Operations Pamphlet No. 42, Supplement No. 1 (India), Brigade Group Dryshod Exercises, 1944 ..	659

Serial No.	Publications.	I. A. O. notifying the issue.
19.	Courses of Instruction (India), 1944, Pamphlet No. 11—Frontier Warfare School, India, Kakul	659
20.	Artillery Training Volume VI—Survey—Pamphlet No. 2, Short Base Flash Spotting, 1943 (For Use by Survey Regiments, R. A.)	659
21.	Coast Artillery Drills, Part III, Pamphlet No. 10A—Gun Drill and Fire Control for 12-Pr. 12 Cwt. Gun on H. A./L. A. Marks VIII* and IX Mountings, 1943 .	659
22.	Preliminary Instructions for Radio Receivers B. C.-312-M and B. C.-342-M, Manufactured by R. C. A. Manufacturing Company, Inc	659
23.	Apparatus A. F. Telegraph (Speech + Duplex)—Working Instructions	659
24.	Preliminary Instructions for Switchboard B. D.-71 and Switchboard B. D.-72, Manufactured by Stromberg—Carlson Telephone Manufacturing Co. (D-4294) ..	659
25.	Revised Edition, Preliminary Instructions for Frequency Meter Set SCR-211-N, Manufactured by Philco Corporation, Philadelphia, PA., U. S. A.	659
26.	Signal Training (All Arms) Pamphlet No. 6—Procedure for Transmitting Artillery Fire Orders, 1942 ..	659
27.	Battle Bulletin No. 2—March, 1944	659
28.	Instructions for the Preparation and Disposal of War Diaries, 1944	659

Serial No.	Publications.	I.A.O. notifying cancellation.
	The following Pamphlets are cancelled :—	
1.	The Stiffkey Stick and How to Use It	455
	Military Training Pamphlet No. 1 (India)—Armoured Units in the Field—	
2.	Part I : Characteristics, Roles and Handling of Armoured Divisions, 1941	511
3.	Part II : General Considerations Common to Both Armoured and Light Armoured Units, 1941 ..	511
4.	Part IV : Armoured Battle, 1941	511
5.	Part VIII : Battle Signals, 1942	511
6.	Part IX : Guide to Signal Training Armoured Division, All Units, 1942	511

Serial No.	Amendments.	I.A.O. notifying the issue.
1.	Military Training Pamphlet No. 8 (India) - Air Forces in Support of the Army, Part IV - Airborne Operations General, 1943, Amendments No. 1	254
2.	Small Arms Training Volume I, Pamphlet No. 10 - Infantry Rangefinder, 1937, Modifications for India No. 5..	254
3.	Small Arms Training Volume I, Pamphlet No. 7 (India), 1940, Part I—.303 Inch Vickers Machine Gun, Amendments No. 2	254
4.	Field Engineering Pamphlet No. 11, Part I - Pushing, Loading and Firing, 1942, Amendments No. 1	254
5.	Military Engineering Volume III, Part II, Pamphlet No. 3, Pontoon Bridging (Pontoons Mk. V and Trestles Mk. VII), 1940, Amendments (No. 4)	254
6.	Notes on the Care and Preservation of Ammunition and Explosives in the Field, Part I—Artillery Ammunition, 1941, Modifications for India No. 1	254
7.	Military Training Pamphlet No. 18 (India) - Notes on Driving and Maintenance of Mechanically Propelled Vehicles (Wheeled) 1941, Amendments (No. 2)	461
8.	Small Arms Training Volume I, Pamphlet No. 4—.303-inch Light Machine Gun (India) 1942, Amendments No. 2	461
9.	Small Arms Training Volume I, Pamphlet No. 11 (India) —Pistol, 1942, Amendments No. 1	461
10.	Roman Urdu Small Arms Training Volume I, Pamphlet No. 7—.303-inch Vickers Machine Gun, Part III (India)— Fire Control Support Platoon, 1940, Tarmim No. 1	461
11.	Courses of Instruction, India, Pamphlet No. 3, 1942— School of Artillery (India), Amendment List No. 1	461
12.	Memorandum of the Training of the Artillery in India, Part I (Field Branch), Amendments No. 1	461
13.	Artillery Code 1941, Amendments (No. 3)	461
14.	Coast Artillery Drills Part III, Pamphlet No. 7 - Gun Drill B. L. 6-inch Marks VII and VII* Guns on Mark V Mounting (Land Service) 1942, Amendments (No. 2)..	461
15.	Gun Drill for B.L. 4.5-inch, Mark II Gun on Carriage 4.5-inch Mark I, and B.L. 5.5-inch, Mark III Gun on Carriage 5.5-inch Mark I, 1941, Amendments (No. 4) ..	461
16.	Addendum to Gun Drill for Q.F. 25-Pr. Mark II Gun on Carriage 25-Pr. Mark I, 1941	461
17.	Gun Drill for Ordnance Q.F. 40 mm. Mark I and III on Mounting Q.F. 40 mm. A.A. Marks II, III and IV on Platform A.A. Marks I and II and Holdfast Mark I and Predictor A.A. No. 3, Land Service, 1942 (Modified for India), Amendments (No. 1)	461
18.	Roman Urdu Gun Drill for Q.F. 3.7-inch, Mark II or III Gun, on Mounting Q.F. 3.7-inch A.A. Mark II (Land Service), Provisional, 1939, Amendments Nos. 4 to 6 (Tarmim Nos. 2 to 4)	461

Serial No.	Amendments.	I.A.O. notifying the issue.
19.	Signal Training Pamphlet No. 2, Part IX—Aerials and Frequency Selection for Corps and Divisional Signals; 1943, Amendments (No. 1)	461
20.	Signal Training Pamphlet No. 4—Construction and Maintenance of Lines, Part III—Poled Lines, 1943, Amendments (No. 1)	461
21.	Signal Training (All Arms) Pamphlet No. 5—Signal Procedure, Part I—Procedure for Radio Telephony, 1943, Amendments (No. 1)	461
22.	Military Training Pamphlet No. 4 (India)—Maintenance in Eastern Theatres of War, 1943, Amendments (No. 2)	667
23.	Military Training Pamphlet No. 10 (India)—Concealment and Camouflage, Part 2—Use of Camouflage Equipment, 1942, Amendments (No. 1)	667
24.	Artillery Training Volume III—Field Gunnery, Pamphlet No. 2, Preparation for Opening Fire, 1943, Amendments (No. 1)	667
25.	Artillery Training Volume III—Field Gunnery, Pamphlet No. 3, Part I—Fire Discipline and Observation of Fire, 1942, Amendments (No. 1)	667
26.	Coast Artillery Training Volume I—Training, 1938, Amendments (No. 5)	667
27.	Fire Control and Gun Drill for 6-inch Emergency Batteries on Naval Mountings, 1940, Amendments (No. 3)	667
28.	Artillery Training Volume IV, Part I—A.A. Gunnery, Pamphlet No. 2—Ammunition (Heavy and Light A.A.), 1942, Modifications for India No. 1	667
29.	Coast Artillery Drills, Part II, Pamphlet No. 4—Drill for Artillery Rangefinders Nos. 4 to 10, 1941, Amendments (No. 2)	667
30.	Coast Artillery Drills, Part I, Pamphlet No. 1—The Fortress System of Range Finding and Observation, 1938, Amendments (No. 2) ..	667
31.	Artillery Training, Volume IV, Part I—A.A.-Gunnery, Pamphlet No. 11—System of Fire Control and Observation of Tracer (Light A.A.), 1943, Amendments No. 1.	667
32.	Coast Artillery Drills, Part III, Pamphlet No. 4—Gun Drill B.L. 9.2 inch, Marks X, X^V and X* Guns on Mark VII Mounting (Land Service), 1942, Amendments (No. 1)	667
33.	Coast Artillery Drills, Part III, Pamphlet No. 8—Gun Drill B.L. 6-inch, Marks VII and VII^V Guns on Marks II, IIA and IV* Mountings, Land Service, 1940, Amendments (No. 3).	667
34.	Military Engineering Volume IV, Part I—Demolitions, 1942, Amendments (No. 1)	667
35.	Signal Training Pamphlet No. 4, Part I—General Principles, 1940, Amendments (No. 2)	667

Note—Small Arms Training, Volume I, Pamphlet No. 20—.303 inch Lewis Machine Gun is now out of stock. This pamphlet is not in much demand but occasionally indents are received from units in possession of this weapon for small number of copies.

There will be many units which are not now in possession of the gun, but still hold stocks of the pamphlet. All such units should immediately return all copies of the pamphlet to the Manager of Publications, Civil Lines, Delhi, for issue to other units. This will obviate the necessity for reprint and thus save an appreciable amount of paper.

————

DISTRIBUTION.

Army in India Training Memorandum is issued to all arms of the service at the scale of one copy for each officer.

QUESTIONS FOR THE C. O.

1. In the past month have you sat down alone and reviewed the training accomplished during the last month ? What did you find ? Is your Unit in a rut ? What's the trouble ? Let's do a quick overhaul.

(a) The Senior Officers : are they pulling their weight ? Are they fit mentally and physically for their job ? If not, what are you doing to have them replaced ? Can they absorb new ideas, and carry them out in their companies, squadrons, etc. ?

(b) The Junior Officers : are they fed up ? If so, there's a reason for it. Are they allowed to develop their initiative and improve the training ? Are they being sent on courses ? Are they "passing it on" when they come back to their unit ? Are they kept physically and mentally on their toes ?

(c) The Training : are weapons in good condition ? Are they being used ? What training aids are being used—films, charts, improvised models, etc. ? Have all instructors (officers and N. C. Os.) taken some course on methods of instruction ? Is instruction really first class ? If not, why not ?

(d) The N. C. Os.: what are you doing to develop new ones as replacements ? Do you hold evening classes for them to improve their knowledge and their value as instructors ?

(e) The Administrative end : are you getting the things you need ? Do the men like their meals ? Cleanliness of the Camp ? Is your Q . M. right in the picture, the Q . M. stores working hand in hand with training ?

Well, what is the verdict ? Is the unit improving, the same, or on the down grade ? Remember, Tojo and Hitler wait for no one.

(From A.T.M. Canada).

———

IMPORTANT

Changes in the designation, location, and/or composition of units, which for reasons of security are not known at once, may necessitate a change in the scale of issue of certain pamphlets/publications required by units.

Units will therefore return all surplus pamphlets and publications to the Manager of Publications, Delhi; and will send to the Chief of the General Staff, M. T. 2 (P), G. H. Q. (I), Meerut, a copy of the list of those returned, giving the reasons.

Demands for additional copies of pamphlets already issued should be sent to the Chief of the General Staff, M.T. 2 (P), G.H.Q. (I), Meerut, who will make the necessary arrangements to meet such demands.

Units are also asked to note that any request received by M.T. 2 (P) to alter existing scales of distribution will be treated as firm, and all future distributions of similar pamphlets will be made at the reduced/increased scale.

REGIMENTAL HISTORIES
OF THE BRITISH ARMY

A SELECTION OF N&MP REPRINTED TITLES
ALWAYS AVAILABLE ALWAYS IN PRINT

READ THE REAL HISTORY OF THE SECOND WORLD WAR IN THE
STORIES OF THE REGIMENTS, CORPS, DIVISIONS, & BATTALIONS
THAT FOUGHT IT.

NAVAL & MILITARY PRESS
WWW.NAVAL-MILITARY-PRESS.COM

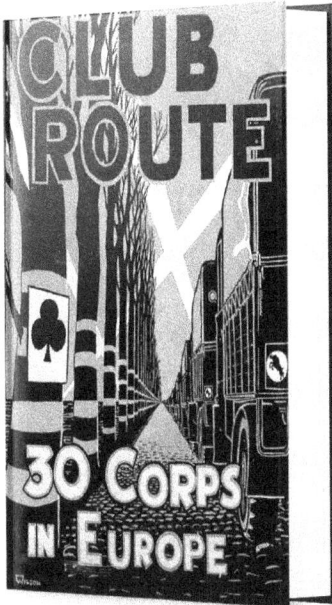

CLUB ROUTE IN EUROPE
The Story of 30 Corps in the European Campaign.
9781783311033

30 Corps was heavily involved in the closing campaigns of the Second World War in Europe, starting when its 50th (Northumbrian) Division landed on Gold Beach on D-day. It helped to clear the Cotentin peninsular in Operation Bluecoat and, after General Brian Horrocks took over command, it took part in Operation Market Garden at Arnhem, and the crossing of the Rhine into the German heartland. A superb unit history of these often difficult and bloody operations.

SEVENTH ARMOURED DIVISION
October 1938 - May 1943
9781474539180

2nd BATTALION SOUTH WALES BORDERS 24th REGIMENT
D-DAY TO VE-DAY
9781474539012

Describing the campaign from D-Day onwards, this excellent contemporary battalion history is divided into two parts. The first contains an outline of the activities of the 2/24th during the campaign in Europe from D-Day to VE-Day, and the second is a detailed narrative of some of the more important actions in which the battalion fought. Complete with a list of awards. Originally printed in Hamburg in 1945.

49 (WEST RIDING) RECONNAISSANCE REGIMENT
Royal Armoured Corps - Summary of Operations June 1944 to May 1945
9781474536677

Rare Reconnaissance unit history that was completed immediately after the war had ended. Following the D-Day invasions, the 49th Reconnaissance Regiment fought as Montgomery's left flank, and played vital roles in the capture of Arnhem, and the liberation of Holland. They are honoured annually in Utrecht to this day. The book is completed with 2 good coloured maps.

THE HISTORY OF THE CORPS OF ROYAL MILITARY POLICE
9781783310951
Excellent history of this corps, almost entirely devoted to WW2 on all fronts, including Middle East, North-West Europe and Burma. Complete with a Roll of Honour.

THE STORY OF THE 79th ARMOURED DIVISION OCTOBER 1942 - JUNE 1945
9781783310395

A magnificent and fully illustrated official history of Britain's 79th Armoured Division - the specialised unit which developed and operated 'Hobart's Funnies', the adapted tanks which carried out a range of tasks on D-day and after ranging from mine clearance to bridge laying. Follows the unit from its formation to victory in Europe.

HISTORY OF THE ARGYLL & SUTHERLAND HIGHLANDERS 7th BATTALION
From El Alamein To Germany
9781781519653

THE ESSEX REGIMENT 1929 - 1950
9781781519813

Comprehensive history of both regular & territorial force battalions, mainly Middle East (inc. Tobruk & Alamein), North-West Europe & 1st Bn. with Chindits in Burma 1944. Rolls of Honour and awards.

HISTORY OF THE IRISH GUARDS IN THE SECOND WORLD WAR
9781474537094

A fine history of a proud regiment; The Irish Guards played their part gallantly during campaigns in Europe, North Africa and Italy during the Second World War, claiming two Victoria Cross recipients during that conflict. The basis of this history was the War Diaries kept by Battalion Intelligence Officers, along with individual records and papers. A Roll of Honour, Honours Awards down to Military Medal, and 22 good maps complete this very good WW2 Regimental.

ALGIERS TO AUSTRIA
The 78th Division in the Second World War
9781783310265

OPERATIONS OF THE EIGHTH CORPS
The River Rhine to the Baltic Sea. A narrative account of the pursuit and final defeat of the German Armed Forces March-May 1945.
9781474538176

THE HISTORY OF THE 51st HIGHLAND DIVISION 1939-1945
9781474536660

The 51st Highland Division fought and lost in France in 1940, was reborn, and fought and won in the North African desert, Sicily and finally in North Western Europe from D-Day to the end of the war. As a division the men earned the respect of friend and foe alike, and this is their story. Amply illustrated with 36 photographs, 18 maps and battle plans (many coloured) that help the reader to follow the course of the conflict. A good index (persons, units and place names) and a statistical battle casualties list complete this good WW2 Divisional History

THE HISTORY OF THE FIFTEENTH SCOTTISH DIVISION 1939-1945
9781783310852

Formed at the outbreak of war in September 1939, the 15th (Scottish) division served in North-western Europe after landing in Normandy soon after D-day on 14 June 1944 . It fought on the Odon River, at Caen, Caumont, Mont Pincon, the Nederrijn, the Rhineland, and across the Rhine. On April 10, 1946, the division was disbanded. The total number of casualties it sustained during the 12 months of fighting was 11,772.

THE STORY OF THE ROYAL ARMY SERVICE CORPS, 1939-1945
9781474538251

A complete history of the RASC in all theatres throughout the Second World War. This a model unit history originally published under the direction of the Institution of the Royal Army Service Corps, it is excellently produced, and arranged by theatre of war. The narrative is full with technical information, and the many photographic plates record visually British military vehicles in service situations.

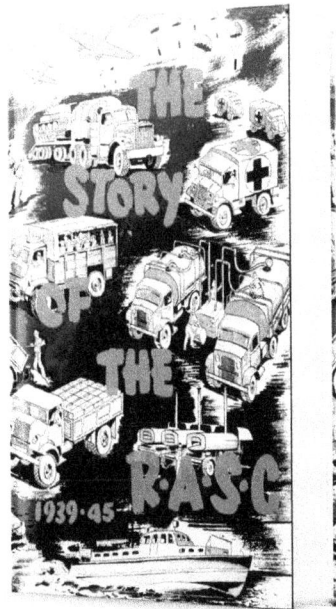

www.ingramcontent.com/pod-product-compliance
Lightning Source LLC
Chambersburg PA
CBHW081516040426
42447CB00013B/3242